The Unloved Dollar Standard

The Unloved Dollar Standard

From Bretton Woods
to the Rise of China

Ronald I. McKinnon

OXFORD
UNIVERSITY PRESS

OXFORD
UNIVERSITY PRESS

Oxford University Press is a department of the
University of Oxford. It furthers the University's objective
of excellence in research, scholarship, and education
by publishing worldwide

Oxford   New York

Auckland   Cape Town   Dar es Salaam   Hong Kong   Karachi
Kuala Lumpur   Madrid   Melbourne   Mexico City   Nairobi
New Delhi   Shanghai   Taipei   Toronto

With offices in

Argentina   Austria   Brazil   Chile   Czech Republic   France   Greece
Guatemala   Hungary   Italy   Japan   Poland   Portugal   Singapore
South Korea   Switzerland   Thailand   Turkey   Ukraine   Vietnam

Oxford is a registered trade mark of Oxford University Press
in the UK and certain other countries

Published in the United States of America by
Oxford University Press
198 Madison Avenue, New York, New York 10016

Library of Congress Cataloging-in-Publication Data
McKinnon, Ronald I.
The unloved dollar standard : from Bretton Woods to the rise of
China / Ronald I. McKinnon.
p.   cm.
Includes bibliographical references and index.
ISBN 978-0-19-993700-4 (cloth : alk. paper)
1. Foreign exchange.   2. Dollar, American.   3. Money—United States.
4. Money—China.   5. Currency question.   6. Currency convertibility.   I. Title.
    HG3851.M44   2013
332.4'560973—dc23   2012018037

1 3 5 7 9 8 6 4 2

Printed in the United States of America
on acid-free paper

To George P. Shultz, the most distinguished American statesman of this age, for his ongoing interest and support despite my contrarian views on the foreign exchanges.

ACKNOWLEDGMENTS

From my 50 years of teaching at Stanford, there are simply too many students to name individually and to disentangle what each has contributed. But collectively they have been invaluable in keeping me moving forward as an international economist. Robert Mundell with his exotic conferences in Santa Columba, and Dominick Salvatore with his annual sessions at the American Economic Association have added to the momentum. Martin Wolf and Charles Goodhart provided keen financial insights. Helen Qiao and Gunther Schnabl have been major contributors to this book, and Zhao Liu helped put the book together. I wish to thank Martin Wolf of the *Financial Times* for constructive criticism and for provoking me to define more clearly the basic model presented in chapter 9. Tim Reichardt and Axel Löffler provided excellent research assistance in support of chapter 12. Margaret McKinnon provided editorial assistance.

CONTENTS

PREFACE

When I started teaching international economics in the early 1960s—the period sometimes called "American high"—the United States bestrode the noncommunist world both politically and economically. Other countries, outside the communist bloc, were anxious to emulate America's wealth-creating institutions. Although the dollar was already the key currency, the legal cover for the postwar international monetary order was the Articles of Agreement of the International Monetary Fund ratified by the principal industrial economies at Bretton Woods, New Hampshire, in 1945. Each member country other than the United States declared a dollar exchange rate parity, while the United States would redeem its Treasury bonds held by foreign *governments* for gold at $35 per ounce.

Because the United States had accumulated almost all the world's gold by the end of World War II, for the next two decades foreign governments were more than happy to hold just U.S. Treasuries in their official reserves. Treasury bonds were interest bearing and more conveniently liquid than gold. In 1945, the United States was the only major country to have broad and deep financial markets without restrictions on currency trading. Without official prompting, the dollar had become the effective key currency used by governments, banks, and private corporations, even before many of the IMF articles were observed in practice. So, very early in the postwar, the dollar became "international money," and the limited gold convertibility constraint on American financial behavior seemed redundant.

Indeed, some influential authors argued early on that the dollar was better than gold, and gold was only attractive because the U.S. Treasury was willing to *buy* as well as sell gold at $35 per ounce. So Emile Despres (1963) argued that gold could be safely demonetized if the United States gradually withdrew from supporting its price. Despres was joined by Charles Kindleberger and Walter Salant to write "The Dollar and World Liquidity: A Minority View" (1966). To best serve the needs of international trade and to provide the rest of the world with international (dollar) liquidity, they essentially argued for a pure dollar standard without any external constraint. In this vein and in a fit of youthful enthusiasm, I wrote "Private and Official International Money: The Case for the Dollar, 1969" for the Princeton *Essays in International Finance*. All these papers presumed that the American monetary and fiscal authorities would better stabilize the American economy and its price level if not hampered by any external constraint—particularly by that barbarous relic, gold.

Amazingly enough, since 1971, when President Nixon officially closed the gold window and so cut what had become just a vestigial tie to gold, the world has remained on an unalloyed dollar standard. The dollar remains the main international unit of account, means of settlement, and official reserve currency. However, it is now clear that the presumption that unfettered U.S. monetary and fiscal policies would lead to macroeconomic stability in the American economy—and by extension to the world economy—was wildly optimistic. This book documents how the many and various monetary and exchange rate shocks emanating from the United States, from the Nixon shock of forced dollar devaluation in 1971 to the zero-interest-rate Bernanke shock of 2008–12, have upset both the American and world economies.

To help overcome the insularity of American policies, I argue that U.S. policymakers should give more weight to stabilizing the dollar's effective (multilateral) exchange rate. Beyond simply reacting to the immediate pressure of inflation or deflation within the domestic American economy, they could lessen the negative impact of U.S. monetary and fiscal policies on other countries by adjusting U.S. interest rates to curb hot money flows to, or from, the United States. America would then be rewarded by positive feedback effects from the world economy that would make the United States itself less inflationary and more stable in the medium and longer terms.

In effect, the center country should pay more (benign) attention to economic events on its "periphery." But the relevant periphery has changed dramatically with the enormous growth of the world economy. When Nixon shuttered the gold window in 1971 and (incorrectly) demanded that other countries appreciate their dollar exchange rates, the relevant "others" were just the individual Western European countries, Japan, and Canada. All had convertible currencies and, beginning in 1970, were deluged with hot money flows anticipating the 1971 dollar devaluation.

After 40 years of more globalized economic growth, however, today's relevant periphery comprises what we now call emerging markets (EMs). These are newly industrializing or diversified primary products producers—such as China or Brazil and many other smaller countries in Asia and Latin America—with mainly convertible currencies. For more than a decade, they have shown high productivity growth that would normally lead to naturally higher domestic interest rates. But if the United States follows a policy of near-zero interest rates, inducing similar ultralow interest rates in the "old" relatively stagnant industrial economies of Europe and Japan, this is a volatile mix. Unless interrupted by banking crises, the stage is set for continual outflows of hot money from the center to the periphery—with losses of monetary control in the emerging markets as their central banks intervene to prevent their currencies from appreciating precipitately. With lags, the resulting worldwide inflation then filters back to the center—as was true of the great inflations of the 1970s.

CHINA

Among today's emerging markets, China is not only the largest but also quite special. I first visited China in 1992 when its currency was largely inconvertible. Hot money inflows or outflows were not a problem, and its trade surplus was insignificant. But the speed of development in light manufacturing, from textiles to consumer electronics, was astonishing—largely the result of intense market competition among enterprises owned by towns, counties, and provinces, as well as by the central government. Local governments were building, or planning to build, large-scale infrastructure in the form of roads, bridges, airports, and so on, even ahead of actual demand for them. The streets were crowded with would-be entrepreneurs, many if not most on bicycles, all seemingly busy with even modest pursuits.

China became the model economy for my 1993 book *The Order of Economic Liberalization: Financial Control in the Transition to a Market Economy*. Instead of a "big bang" approach to escape from the detailed state intervention characteristic of socialist economies, China's approach was one of well-ordered, step-by-step gradualism with the last stage being the elimination of capital controls in the balance of payments. For reasons discussed in this book—as well as in the earlier one—China has yet to finish this last stage.

Although intrigued by China's development, I did not initially connect it with my main line of thought on the world dollar standard. To be sure, China like all emerging markets made good monetary use of the dollar standard in organizing its rapidly growing foreign trade and payments. And when China went from a system of multiple exchange rates to a unified yuan/dollar rate in 1994, followed in 1996 by current-account convertibility, this became the much-needed anchor for its price level and financial system more generally. But I did not think then that China today would become, albeit inadvertently, a *pillar* of the world dollar standard.

China's supporting role arises in large part from its own strength—very high domestic saving leading to huge domestic and, more recently, foreign investments so that the ambit of its dollar-based foreign trade is now the world's largest. But over the past decade, China's saving has exceeded domestic investment, while saving in the United States has dipped below its domestic investment. The result is China's decade-long trade surplus, which is largely bilateral with the saving-deficient United States. The resulting trade (saving) imbalance floods the United States with Chinese manufactures that lead to political friction in the form of "China bashing," which is made worse by so-called informed U.S. opinion misdiagnosing the problem as one of China undervaluing it dollar exchange rate.

However, in becoming the world's largest creditor country (by some measures) and creditor of the United States, China is also an *immature creditor*. The renminbi is still a long distance from being an international currency like the dollar in part because China's domestic financial markets are still subject to exchange controls and interest rate restrictions (see Prasad and Ye 2012). This financial immaturity means that China cannot finance its huge saving surplus by building up RMB claims on foreigners, but must resort to illiquid direct investments abroad or to acquiring liquid *dollar* claims on foreigners. But Chinese banks and insurance companies are inhibited from holding liquid dollar claims as assets when their domestic financial liabilities are in RMB. Because of this currency mismatch, China cannot free its foreign exchange market or float its exchange rate—and the government is trapped into being the principal financial intermediary for financing the trade surplus.

This trap is bearable as long as China keeps the yuan/dollar rate fairly stable, and successfully resists pushes by American China bashing to let it continually appreciate. But the need for a modus vivendi between the two giants in the world economy is clear.

As China has gained in size and strength over the last thirty years, so has America been diminished by very low saving from large and growing fiscal deficits. In addition, inward-looking monetary policy by the U.S. Federal Reserve Bank, with its current policy of keeping short-term interest rates close to zero being a prime example, hurts the world economy as well as the American one. Financial repression in China is now a problem because the Fed forces it to keep its internal interest rates too low.

But there is a parallel threat to the American economy. If emerging markets, of which China is the largest and natural leader, tire or become exasperated with continually buying dollar assets at next to no interest in order to prevent their currencies from appreciating, collectively they might stop. True, their currencies would then all appreciate against the dollar. But as long as they did so together, no one EM's exports need be relatively disadvantaged. However, the collective effect of withdrawing support for the U.S. balance of payments would be to uncover the large U.S. fiscal deficit. The result would be a traumatic credit crunch within the American economy as U.S. banks bought Treasuries rather than lending normally to business firms—as happened in a more minor way in the so-called U.S. credit crunch of 1991–92.

To prevent a sharp downturn in China's biggest export market and possible collapse in the dollar standard itself, the two countries should work together for better mutual understanding of what needs to change. If both American and Chinese policymakers would read this book, it would be a step in the right direction.

Stanford, 2012

The Unloved Dollar Standard

CHAPTER 1

༅༅

Introduction

The Unloved Dollar Standard

The world dollar standard is an accident of history that greatly facilitates international trade and exchange—even trade not directly involving the United States. Since 1945, the dollar has been the key currency for clearing international payments among banks, including interventions by governments to set exchange rates; the dominant currency for invoicing trade in primary commodities; and the principal currency in official exchange reserves.

Although the strong network effects of the dollar standard greatly increase the financial efficiency of multilateral trade (ch. 2), nobody loves it. Erratic U.S. monetary and exchange rate policies since the late 1960s have made, and still make, foreigners unhappy. A weak and falling dollar led to the worldwide price inflations of the 1970s and contributed to the disastrous asset bubbles and global credit crisis after 2000—including the global credit crunch of 2008–9. Dollar weakness aggravated the postwar world's three great oil shocks in 1973, 1979, and 2007–8 (ch. 4).

The U.S. Federal Reserve Bank's current policy of keeping short-term interest rates near zero and out of alignment with

higher interest rates in emerging markets on the dollar standard's periphery makes the international monetary system vulnerable to "carry" trades. For more than two years after 2008, a
flood of hot money into the periphery caused a loss of monetary
control, commodity bubbles, and worldwide inflation (ch. 5).
Then, in August 2011, these inflows into emerging markets suddenly reversed. A new worldwide banking crisis, associated with
the possible breakdown of the euro, cut off the flow of credit to
businesses everywhere—but particularly to highly leveraged
carry traders. When these carry-trade bubbles suddenly unwind,
they can result in huge swings in exchange rates as well as credit
crunches. No wonder that foreigners—from the French in the
late 1960s to the Chinese since 2008—have called for a new
international monetary regime that is not so dependent on the
vicissitudes of any one national currency, that is, the U.S. dollar.

The asymmetrical nature of the dollar standard also makes
many Americans unhappy because they cannot control their own
exchange rate. Under the rules of the dollar standard game as
explained in chapters 2 and 3, foreign governments may opt to
set their exchange rates against the dollar—while, to prevent
conflict, the U.S. government typically does not intervene.
Nevertheless, Americans often complain that foreigners set their
dollar exchange rates unfairly. American Japan bashing from
the late 1970s to the mid-1990s over the alleged undervaluation
of the yen, and China bashing in the new millennium over the
alleged undervaluation of the renminbi, are two cases in point.

So we have the great paradox. Although nobody loves the dollar
standard, the revealed preference of both governments and
private participants in the foreign exchange markets since 1945
has been to continue to use it. As the principal monetary mechanism ensuring that international trade remains robustly multilateral rather than narrowly bilateral, it is a remarkable survivor
that is too valuable to lose and too difficult to replace.

With the advent of the euro on January 1, 1999, and with the
GNP of the euro area being (slightly) greater than that of the

United States, it was once thought that the more stable-valued euro would gradually supplant the central role of the dollar in international finance. And the euro has served as international money in Europe's own backyard in smaller countries to its east and in a few former colonies in Africa and elsewhere. However, the Greek debt crisis of 2010 heralded a new era of grave doubts regarding the euro's survival in its present form. In late 2011, virtually all the sovereign bonds of countries in the euro zone became suspect. Beyond this, the international competitiveness of the weaker "Club Med" countries continued to deteriorate, making debt repayment problematic. Thus the prospect of the euro becoming a truly international reserve currency beyond Europe is greatly diminished.

Since 1980, China's astonishing GDP growth based on its transition to a market-based system has propelled it to become the world's biggest trading economy, as measured (in dollars of course!) by the sum of its exports and imports. With its huge population, China's domestic GNP is already comparable to that of the larger European countries—and has overtaken slow-growing Japan. Within a decade or so, China's GNP could well become larger than that of the United States itself.

Chinese officials, such as Governor Zhou Xiaochuan of the People's Bank of China (PBC), bemoan the use of one national currency as "international money," a practice they regard as increasingly anomalous.

The People's Bank of China released a statement by Zhou Xiaochuan, on March 23, 2009. It calls for replacing the dollar as the dominant world currency and creating "an international reserve currency that is disconnected from individual nations and is able to remain stable in the long run." The domestic monetary needs of the center country, Zhou contends plausibly, are increasingly likely to diverge from those of the rest of the world as globalization proceeds. China nervously sits on more than $3 trillion in official dollar exchange reserves and is effectively trapped into acquiring more because of its exchange rate objectives in the face of America's zero-interest-rate policy (ch. 5).

Like Japan's earlier attempts in the 1980s and 1990s to "internationalize" the yen, in the new millennium China has taken steps to subsidize the partial internationalization of the renminbi (RMB). Its government encourages trade on its immediate borders to be invoiced in RMB, and has loosened capital controls—at least on outflows. In principle, Shanghai could become an international center for financing China's large trade (saving) surplus in RMB—as Germany now finances its large trade (saving) surplus in euros. These steps are all well and good in potentially reducing currency mismatches within China's economy (ch. 11).

However, the dollar has two great advantages for retaining its central role as international money, advantages that will persist even when China's economy becomes bigger than that of the United States.

First, having just one dominant international money is a natural monopoly. Introducing a second or third reserve currency would raise the transactions costs of making and clearing international payments among diverse countries the world over (ch. 2). True, for subsets of countries that trade intensively with one another and are perhaps contiguous (such as those in, or potentially in) the euro zone, the efficiency gains from having stable intrazone exchange rates from using a common European currency are sufficiently high to offset any network losses in dollar-based trade with the rest of the world. But not so otherwise.

Second, there is a tremendous first-mover advantage to the national currency already ensconced as international money. Once the private conventions of exchange (networks) are set so that most banks use the dollar as the intermediary currency in money changing between second and third currencies, transactions costs fall in these dollar-based markets as their liquidity increases. With this fall in costs, the remaining banks are attracted in to use the dollar—and costs fall even further from economies of an ever larger network as globalization proceeds.

Moreover, once established as international money, the dollar has become a "safe haven" in times of great international crises—even ones emanating from the United States itself. In the credit crunch and global downturn of 2008 from the U.S. subprime mortgage crisis, the resulting flight to safety sharply lifted the foreign exchange value of the dollar against most other currencies that were not tied to it. In the great euro banking crisis that began in 2011, there was another surge in the demand for dollars that was felt mainly as a sudden reversal of hot money flows into emerging markets—such as China and Brazil. But it is too early to tell how this latest crisis will play itself out.

Although "black swans" are not entirely out of the question, only a cataclysmic financial event could now displace the dollar as first mover. The financial earthquakes of the 1970s and 80s, and then after 2000—with the dollar at their epicenters—have, amazingly enough, left the facilitating role of today's world dollar standard intact (ch. 2). Notwithstanding the dollar's robustness as a facilitator in surviving the calamities of the last few decades, its performance as the world's monetary anchor has become abysmal (chs. 4 and 5). Why should this be the case?

THE INSULAR TRADITION IN U.S. MONETARY POLICY

Since 1945, American monetary policy has remained inward looking even as the process of globalization has made such insularity obsolete (ch. 3)—the central theme in this book. By continuing to pursue insular domestic monetary and financial policies while neglecting feedback effects from the rest of the world, the United States itself has often been the biggest loser. And the negative consequences of this insularity have been compounded by U.S. policymakers being in thrall to successive macroeconomic and foreign exchange fallacies—listed at the end of this chapter—leading to policy mistakes.

What is the historical origin of today's insularity in conducting U.S. monetary policy? For more than two decades after 1945, the American Gulliver dominated the noncommunist financial world. Moreover, globalization in the form of freely flowing international finance—as we now know it—was only nascent. Outside of the United States, controls on international capital flows in both the industrial and developing economies proliferated—the legacy of war and depression. The United States—with its relatively open financial system that made, and still makes, the dollar attractive as international money—was then insulated from financial shocks elsewhere.

Under this early dollar standard, insularity in the conduct of American monetary policy, where the Fed looked only at U.S. domestic economic indicators—such as the rate of inflation, unemployment, or the financial positions of American banks—was roughly correct (ch. 3). Useful monetary feedback through the foreign exchanges to the U.S. monetary authority was small or nonexistent. Foreign currencies were not rival stores of international liquidity, and international hot money flows were minimal. As long as the U.S. price level and financial system could be stabilized independently, other countries could take that as a datum and anchor their own macro policies by pegging to it. The Fed's "benign neglect" of macroeconomic conditions in the rest of the noncommunist world was the best policy.

However, times change. By the mid-1960s, Western Europe and Japan had returned to currency convertibility on current account, a necessary ingredient for their strong economic growth led by the rapid expansion of world trade. In addition, controls on flows of financial capital had pretty well eroded by the end of the 1970s. West Germany was the leader. It effectively eliminated capital controls in the late 1960s with a single-minded determination to keep German inflation lower than that of the United States. Through international currency substitution, the potential for short-term hot money flows was now in place.

However, if the U.S. had followed a policy of domestic price-level and exchange rate stability, even after abrogating its commitment to gold convertibility in the late 1960s (ch. 3), the credibility of traditional dollar exchange parities from the 1960s could well have been sustained. Then capital-account liberalization by countries on the dollar's periphery would not have been a problem. Instead of the hot money flows we see today, international money flows would make exchange rates more stable—in the mode of Milton Friedman's (1953) hypothetical stabilizing speculators.

But it was the American government itself—concerned with declining competitiveness of U.S. industry in world markets—that upset the credibility apple cart. In the well-known "Nixon shock" of August 1971 (ch. 4), the U.S. president ended America's gold convertibility commitment and imposed a temporary tariff on imports of manufactures until governments in the other industrial counties agreed to appreciate substantially against the dollar. ("Emerging markets" as we know them today were not yet economically significant on the world scene.) Less well remembered is the follow-up "Carter shock" of 1977, where Treasury secretary Michael Blumenthal was co-opted into talking the dollar down further, particularly against the yen. The expectation of the Treasury's actions set off another hot money run out of the United States, with a sharply falling dollar in 1977–78. This only ended when an international consortium of central banks intervened to prop up the dollar in October 1978, with a sharp increase in U.S. interest rates lasting into the early 1980s.

In both the Nixon and Carter cases, it was the *ex ante* expectation that the dollar would depreciate (a one-way bet), more than the *ex post* fact of depreciation, that set off hot money outflows from the United States. Acting individually, foreign central banks in Western Europe, Japan, and Canada tried to resist excessive exchange appreciation against the world's central money by intervening to buy dollars with domestic base money. The resulting explosions in "world" money in 1970–72 and in 1977–78 led to the two great inflationary episodes of the 1970s, which eventually engulfed the United States itself (ch. 4).

In retrospect, the monetary-cum–foreign exchange origins of the inflations of the 1970s from runs on the dollar have been obscured by the popular tendency to explain them away as caused by two exogenous oil shocks—interruptions in the supply of crude oil from the Middle East. However, chapter 4 also shows that the sharp increases in the price of oil in 1974 and again in 1979 *followed* the prior losses of monetary control, and were much larger than could be explained by sudden oil supply constraints from the Yom Kippur War in September 1973 or the Iranian revolution in 1979.

This contrarian view is bolstered by the more recent experience from 2002 to July 2008 of a falling dollar. With relatively low U.S. interest rates, a dollar carry trade (short-term capital outflows) induced bubbles in many commodity and real estate markets worldwide, culminating in a sharp spike in the price of oil in the first half of 2008, which was proportionately as large as the two spikes in the 1970s (ch. 4). But this more recent episode was not associated with any sudden "exogenous" shock or politically motivated disruption in the supply of oil in world markets. Thus the monetary expansion–cum–falling dollar explanation of the earlier oil price spikes seems vindicated by the recent spike in the first half of 2008.

In retrospect, it seems obvious (at least to the author!) that past runs on the dollar, in anticipation of ongoing depreciations, gave ample advance warning to the Fed that something was amiss. Inflation in goods or asset prices was likely to follow unless the Fed tightened up to stop the rot. Conversely, the few cases where the dollar appreciated sharply—as in 1984 into 1985 so as to create the industrial "rust bowl" in the American Midwest—the strong dollar signaled that U.S. monetary policy was too tight.

If the Federal Reserve's monetary policy had been less insular, say by giving more weight to smoothing fluctuations in the dollar's effective exchange rate, both the rest of the world and the United States itself would have been the beneficiaries. But the technical specifics of having the Fed behave more appropriately as the de facto central banker for the world are tricky, and are not spelled out until chapter 13.

THE LENDER OF LAST RESORT IN A DOLLAR-BASED SYSTEM

To be sure, in crisis circumstances, the U.S. Fed or Treasury has willingly lent dollars to foreign governments in distress—as with the subprime mortgage crisis of 2007–08 and the euro crisis of 2011–12. The principal financial vehicle for doing this is for the Fed to swap dollars with a foreign central bank for its currency—in effect a collateralized loan. Then the foreign central bank can lend the dollars to its domestic commercial banks so they can make good on their dollar obligations in times of stress— when the demand for dollars as a safe haven has suddenly escalated.

For smaller developing countries in the postwar, the United States has delegated crisis lending (mainly in dollars) to the International Monetary Fund. The IMF has become the world's crisis lender of "first resort." But when a crisis is sufficiently acute to outrun the immediate dollar resources of the IMF, then the U.S. government supplements it in one way or another—as with the great Asian crisis of 1997–98 or the Mexican crisis of 1994–95, or the euro crisis currently, where central bank swaps with the Fed supplement direct IMF lending.

Despite being the lender of last resort in international crisis situations, however, the Fed still does not bend the mainline stance of U.S. domestic monetary policy—by easing or tightening— to what is going on in the international economy. In succeeding chapters, I will contend that this is, and has been, the most serious lacuna in the world's monetary system.

MACROECONOMIC FALLACIES

If this prima facie case for a more outward-looking U.S. domestic monetary policy is granted, what has inhibited, and still inhibits, the Fed from overcoming its traditional insularity?

Three macroeconomic fallacies, some but not all of which have been exposed as such, have undermined monetary stability in the U.S. and world economies:

1. *The Phillips Curve Fallacy.* In the late 1960s, mild inflation broke out in the United States from the government failing to finance properly the Vietnam War and domestic social expenditures. With fixed dollar exchange parities, American industries became less competitive from the moderate increase in the U.S. price level. But disinflation was inhibited for fear of increasing unemployment—the then prevalent belief in the Phillips Curve. Instead of disinflating, the U.S. government insisted that the countries of Western Europe and Japan all appreciate their exchange rates against the dollar: the infamous Nixon shock of 1971, as discussed further in chapter 4.

2. *The Efficient Markets Fallacy.* The bursting of price bubbles in asset markets—common stocks, residential real estate, primary commodities—over the last decade has punctured the once common belief, firmly held by Alan Greenspan when he was chairman of the U.S. Fed from 1987 to 2008, that asset markets are self-correcting and can be safely ignored by the monetary authority—at least until a bubble bursts. Although the possibility of bubbles and herdlike behavior is now well recognized in attempts to regulate domestic finance, this disillusion has yet to encompass the foreign exchange markets per se—where wild swings in floating exchange rates often arise out of carry trades that have bubblelike characteristics. Most economists still believe that freely floating exchange rates are the preferred "market" solution.

3. *The Exchange Rate and Trade Balance Fallacy.* The most enduring fallacy inhibiting many governments, but particularly that of the United States, from orienting monetary policy toward exchange stability is the presumption that the exchange rate should be assigned to correcting trade (net saving) imbalances across counties. In particular, if creditor countries such as China are persuaded or coerced to appreciate against the dollar, conventional wisdom has it that their trade surpluses will be reduced. But this is not true in a world where finance and investment have become "globalized"—see the chapters 6 through 9 on trade imbalances in general, and chapters 10 through 12 on China in particular.

Although fallacies 1 and 2 are in abeyance, this exchange rate–cum–trade balance fallacy is alive and well—witness the several attempts by the U.S. government since 1970 to talk the dollar down. Despite protestations that the government really wants a "strong" dollar, today's weak dollar is tolerated because influential economists still believe that dollar devaluation will reduce America's trade deficit—the belief that motivates the bashing of China to appreciate the renminbi against the dollar. This third fallacy is particularly pernicious for global monetary stability when the center country in the world's monetary system tries to depreciate its own currency. It remains the greatest conceptual barrier to having a more internationalist, outward-looking, and thus more stable U.S. monetary policy.

Even so, the dollar standard remains remarkably resilient. The succeeding chapters provide historical and analytical perspectives on the different phases of the postwar dollar standard in order to better understand this resilience despite the great volatility—past and present—in the global monetary system.

PART I

The International Money Machine

CHAPTER 2

❧

The U.S. Dollar's Facilitating Role as International Money Today

Why does the dollar's asymmetrical role in facilitating international exchange continue today even when the other industrial countries—such as Japan and those in Europe—have recovered from World War II, and no longer have exchange controls or closed capital markets? A little algebra helps explain continued dollar predominance. Suppose there are 150 national currencies in the world economy. To facilitate international exchange, the markets themselves would always pick just one as the central money. The reason is a big economy in the number of foreign exchange markets.

Consider a world of N countries with independent national monies. From basic probability theory, the total number of country pairs in the system is the combination of N things taken two at a time ($^{N}C_{2}$). If foreign exchange dealers tried to trade within each pair, say, Swedish crowns against Australian dollars, or Korean won against Japanese yen, the number of bilateral markets would be huge, that is, $N(N - 1) / 2$. With 150 national currencies in the world ($N = 150$), and dealers tried to trade each pair, there would be 11,175 foreign exchange markets!

It is expensive for any bank to set up a foreign exchange trading desk. Thus, rather than trading all pairs of currencies bilaterally, in practice just one currency, the Nth, is chosen as the central vehicle currency. Then all trading and exchange takes place first against the vehicle currency before going to the others. By having all currency trading against that one currency, the number of markets in the system can be reduced to $N - 1$. Thus, with 150 countries, there need be just 149 independent foreign exchange markets—instead of 11,175! Unlike the Bretton Woods system, where member countries set official dollar parities, this theorem does not depend on any formal agreement among governments. In private markets today, choosing one currency like the dollar to be the intermediary is the most natural way of economizing on foreign exchange transacting.

Once the $N - 1$ foreign exchange rates are established against the Nth (central) currency, triangular arbitrage with this central money becomes sufficient to establish all the relevant cross rates between any pair of nondollar currencies (McKinnon 1979). Once the 149 primary dollar exchange rates are established, triangular arbitrage (among banks) becomes sufficient to establish all the remaining 11,175 cross rates. In thinly traded exchange markets involving small countries, many of these cross rates will be only notional—although still effective as guides for importers and exporters. But history is important. If one country starts off providing the central money, as the United States in the late 1940s did, then it becomes a natural monopoly because of the economies of scale. The more countries that deal in dollars, the cheaper it is for them all to deal in dollars. If you're a Japanese importer of Swedish Volvos and you want to pay for the Volvos, you first get your bank to convert your yen into dollars on the open interbank market, then use the dollars to buy Swedish kronor. The Volvo Corporation is paid in Swedish kronor, and the Japanese importer gets the Volvos. However, the dollar is the intermediary interbank currency.

Box 2.1

THE U.S. DOLLAR'S FACILITATING ROLE AS
INTERNATIONAL MONEY SINCE 1945

	Private	*Official*
Medium of exchange	Vehicle	Intervention
Store of value	Banking	Reserves
Unit of account	Invoice	Peg
Standard of deferred payment	Private bonds	Sovereign bonds

Using the standard textbook classification of the roles of money, box 2.1 summarizes our paradigm of the dollar's central role in facilitating international exchange. For both the private and government sectors, the dollar performs as medium of exchange, store of value, unit of account, and standard of deferred payment for international transacting on current and capital account—as it has done since 1945.

First, the dollar is a *medium of exchange*. Because the foreign exchange markets are mainly interbank, the dollar is the vehicle currency in interbank transactions serving customers in the private sector. Thus, when any government—usually represented by its central bank—intervenes to influence its exchange rate, it also finds it cheaper and more convenient to use the dollar as the official intervention currency. (The major exception to this convention is a fringe of small European countries east of the euro zone that mainly use the euro as their central money.)

Following Peter Kenen (2002), tables 2.1 through 2.6 analyze the dollar's asymmetrical role in international finance. Table 2.1 shows that the dollar is on one side or the other of 85 to 90 percent of interbank foreign exchange transactions worldwide.

Remember that the dollar's dominance in international trade is limited to the interbank market, that is, money changing among banks. For the most part, the dollar does not encroach on purely domestic monetary transactions among households and

Table 2.1. CURRENCIES INVOLVED IN FOREIGN EXCHANGE TRADING
(PERCENTAGE OF GLOBAL TRADING, COUNTING EACH TRADE TWICE)

Currency	1998	2001	2004	2007	2010
Dollar	86.8	89.9	88.0	85.6	84.9
EMS currencies and euro[a]	52.5	37.9	37.4	37.0	39.1
Yen	21.7	23.5	20.8	17.2	19.0
Pound	11.0	13.0	16.5	14.9	12.9
Swiss franc	7.1	6.0	6.0	6.8	6.4
Canadian and Australian dollar	6.5	8.8	10.2	10.9	12.9
All other currencies	14.4	20.9	21.1	27.6	24.8
Memorandum Total turnover in $billion	**1,705**	**1,505**	**2,040**	**3,370**	**3,981**

Source: Bank for International Settlements, Central Bank Survey of Foreign Exchange and Derivative Market Activity in April 2010: Preliminary Results (September 2010).
Note: As each trade involves two currencies, each trade is counted twice, so percentages should add up to 200, but detail may not sum to total because of rounding.
[a] European Monetary System (EMS) currencies include the ecu and Danish krone.

firms. These are almost always in the domestic currency.[1] And if the interbank market is not limited by foreign exchange controls, most firms and households need to hold liquid balances in just their domestic currency—from which their banks make foreign payments intermediated through the dollar.

Beyond spot transacting, however, the interbank market is multidimensional in forward foreign exchange. To serve exporters who want to sell future foreign exchange earnings, or importers who anticipate having to pay foreign exchange, dealers in the major banks remain open to transact with each other and their nonbank customers at virtually every term to maturity. Thus, with a liquid "wholesale" interbank market where banks whose names are taken without question by counterparties, any bank can easily cover an open forward exchange position thrust upon it by its "retail" nonbank customers.

By having most interbank transactions funneled through the dollar as the intermediary currency, this high trading density with its high liquidity is precisely what the dollar standard provides. Purely bilateral forward exchange markets would be thinly traded and hopelessly illiquid. In contrast, banks in more liquid dollar-based markets have much less trouble matching buy and sell orders at different maturities, and so see less risk. Thus they offer much lower bid-asked spreads, or lower brokerage fees, in forward transacting with other banks and with their nonbank customers.

Notice that, apart from the absence of foreign exchange controls, country size matters. Because in 1945, the United States had by far the largest GDP and foreign trade sector, interbank trading in dollars against other currencies was naturally more dense and so more liquid. True, the global economy has grown enormously since then, and the American economy—while still the largest—has shrunk relative to its major trading partners.[2]

Yet, paradoxically, this global growth—particularly in Asia— seems to have strengthened dollar dominance. Because rapidly growing Asian and Latin American economies clear interbank payments in dollars, say in trade between China and Brazil, the liquidity of dollar-based foreign exchange markets is enhanced— leading to further declines in bank transaction fees. Even though the relative size of the American economy itself is declining, the ambit of dollar-based interbank exchanges is increasing—thus preserving the dollar standard into the indefinite future.

Perhaps counterintuitively, table 2.2 shows that dollar-based foreign exchange transacting is not centered geographically in the United States. Although the dollar is the predominant money in foreign currency trading, London has the biggest foreign exchange markets using the dollar as the clearing currency. The United Kingdom actually has the bigger proportion of foreign exchange trading. Offshore markets exist in Singapore and Hong Kong.

Table 2.2. GEOGRAPHIC DISTRIBUTION OF FOREIGN EXCHANGE TRADING
(PERCENTAGE OF GLOBAL TRADING)

Country	1998	2001	2004	2007	2010
United Kingdom	32.6	32.0	32.0	34.6	36.7
United States	18.3	16.1	19.1	17.4	17.9
Euro zone countries	17.0	14.6	13.1	10.5	9.4
Germany	4.7	5.4	4.6	2.4	2.1
France	3.7	2.9	2.6	3.0	3.0
Others	8.6	6.2	5.9	5.2	4.3
Japan	7.0	9.0	8.0	5.8	6.2
Singapore	6.9	6.1	5.1	5.6	5.3
Switzerland	4.4	4.5	3.3	5.9	5.2
Hong Kong	3.8	4.0	4.1	4.2	4.7
All others	10.1	13.6	15.3	15.8	14.7

Source: Bank for International Settlements, Central Bank Survey of Foreign Exchange and Derivative Market Activity in April 2010: Preliminary Results (September 2010).
Note: Details may not sum to total because of rounding.

In attempting to "internationalize" the renminbi (RMB), the People's Bank of China has tried to encourage offshore trading in RMB in Hong Kong since 2010. But this attempt is handicapped by China's controls on capital inflows designed to prevent or slow hot money flows from dollars into RMB. So RMB purchased by U.S. dollars in Hong Kong don't appear to be convertible into mainland RMB—but the jury is still out on whether this new policy succeeds.

Referring back to box 2.1, we note that the dollar is also an international *store of value*. Corporations and some individuals hold dollar bank accounts in London, Singapore, and other offshore banking centers—as well as in the United States itself. But it is virtually impossible to obtain data on the distribution of foreign exchange holdings by currency of denomination for the private sector the world over. It is estimated that more than half the stock of coin and currency issued by the U.S. government circulates abroad in Latin America, Russia, and in Africa and other financially distressed areas. So too does the euro circulate as hand-to-hand currency outside of the euro zone, but more in the smaller countries of Eastern Europe. However, the Bank for International Settlements does compile information on the cross-border liabilities of reporting banks identifiable by currency, and this is shown in table 2.3.

As the store of value of governments, international exchange reserves are mainly in dollars—as shown in table 2.4. After the advent of the euro, in 1999, many economists suggested that foreign central banks were going to start diversifying their official reserve exchange reserves into euros. Thus the dollar standard would not be as strong. Table 2.4 shows that the degree of this diversification has been minor. In developing countries, about two-thirds of their exchange reserves are in dollars if you allocate their unspecified exchange reserves in table 2.4 in the same way that the specified reserves are distributed. The developing countries used to hold some deutsche marks, francs, and pounds sterling. Now, the euro is held more or less in the same balance as were the old European national currencies. So even before the global crisis of 2008, the euro did not encroach much on the dollar-based system. After the great euro crisis that began in 2011, however, the euro's worldwide role seems destined to shrink rather than to expand.

Third, the dollar serves as a *unit of account* for much of international trade. Trade in primary commodities shows a strong pattern of using the dollar as the main currency of *invoice* (McKinnon 1979). Exports of homogeneous primary products such as oil, wheat, soybeans, iron ore, and copper all tend to be invoiced in dollars, with worldwide price formation (quotations) in a centralized exchange. Futures markets for hedging price risk in each commodity are located at these centralized exchanges—which are usually in American cities such as Chicago and New York, although dollar-denominated commodity exchanges do exist in London and elsewhere.

Table 2.3. CROSS-BORDER LIABILITIES OF BANKS (PERCENTAGE OF GLOBAL TOTAL IDENTIFIABLE BY CURRENCY)

Currency	1998	1999	2000	2001	2002	2003	2004	2005	2006	2007	2008	2009	2010
Dollar	47.6	50.9	52.5	53.5	48.7	46.5	45.2	47.7	47.6	44.7	45.3	45.5	46.9
Euro zone currencies and euro	26.3	26.3	25.1	26.2	30.5	33.8	35.4	33.4	33.0	34.2	34.8	35.0	33.3
Yen	8.4	7.6	7.1	5.0	5.1	4.1	3.9	3.7	3.0	3.6	4.4	3.4	3.7
Pound	6.5	6.6	6.4	7.2	7.3	7.8	7.8	7.5	8.2	9.3	7.3	7.1	6.4
Swiss franc	3.2	2.8	2.5	2.7	2.5	2.2	2.0	1.8	1.7	1.6	1.8	1.7	1.7
Other	8.1	5.7	6.3	5.4	6.0	5.7	5.7	5.9	6.5	6.7	6.5	7.3	8.0
Total allocated liabilities in $billion	8,399	8,652	9,521	10,244	12,112	14,552	17,203	18,945	23,396	30,177	27,904	26,929	27,060

Source: Bank for International Settlements, BIS Quarterly Review.
Note: Details may not sum to total because of rounding.

Table 2.4. CURRENCY COMPOSITION OF OFFICIAL FOREIGN EXCHANGE
RESERVES (PERCENTAGE OF GLOBAL TOTAL)

Country Group and Currency	2000	2002	2004	2006	2008	2010
Industrial Countries						
Dollar	69.8	66.5	67.3	68.2	67.2	64.4
Euro zone currencies and euro	18.4	23.2	22.8	22.1	23.1	24.3
Yen	7.3	5.4	5.0	4.3	4.3	4.7
Pound	2.8	2.8	2.7	3.3	2.7	2.6
Other and unspecified	1.8	2.1	2.3	2.1	2.7	4.0
Developing Countries:						
Dollar	74.8	68.6	63.0	61.5	60.7	58.4
Euro zone currencies and euro	18.1	25.3	29.2	29.5	30.0	28.3
Yen	2.7	1.7	1.3	1.3	1.9	2.4
Pound	2.6	2.8	4.9	6.0	5.4	6.3
Other and unspecified	1.7	1.7	1.5	1.7	2.0	4.6

Source: International Monetary Fund, Annual Report 2004.
Note: Details may not sum to total because of rounding. Euro zone currencies include the deutsche mark,
French franc, and Dutch guilder, as well as ecu held by industrial countries.

Invoicing patterns for exports of manufactured goods are more
complex (McKinnon 1979). Major industrial countries with
strong currencies tend to invoice their exports in their home currencies. Before the European Monetary Union (EMU), more than
75 percent of German exports had been invoiced in marks, more
than 50 percent of French exports invoiced in francs, and so on.
But these illustrative ratios were dominated by intra-European
trade. With the advent of the EMU, how much continental
European countries will invoice their exports outside of Europe
in euros remains unknown. But for manufactured goods, the

proportion of euro invoicing probably corresponds to the proportion of deutsche mark invoicing that Germany used before the euro.

Within Asia, however, foreign trade is invoiced mainly in dollars. Since we lack general information on the invoicing practices of most Asian countries, table 2.5 displays invoicing practices for just Korea—itself now a fairly industrialized economy. In 2006, about 82.9 percent of Korean imports and 84.5 percent of exports were invoiced in U.S. dollars.

In striking contrast, yen invoicing in Korean trade is surprisingly small. In 2006, table 2.5 shows, only 4.7 percent of Korean exports and 10.5 percent of Korean imports were invoiced in yen. Korea has traditionally be a big importer of capital goods from Japan. Table 2.5 also shows that the use of European currencies is negligible.

Because the smaller Asian economies are less industrialized than Korea, their currencies are even less likely to be used in foreign trade. China is the big unknown. But the lack of openness in its domestic financial markets and use of exchange controls on capital account suggest that the proportion of dollar invoicing in China's trade is even greater than in Korea's. For smaller East

Table 2.5.   INVOICE CURRENCIES IN KOREAN TRADE, 1980–2006 (PERCENT)

	Exports (receipts)					Imports (payments)				
	$	¥	DMª	£	Other	$	¥	DMª	£	Other
1980	96.1	1.2	2.0	0.4	0.3	93.2	3.7	1.7	0.5	0.9
1985	94.7	3.7	0.6	0.3	0.7	82.4	12.3	2.0	0.5	2.8
1990	88.0	7.8	2.1	0.5	1.7	79.1	12.7	4.1	0.9	3.4
1995	88.1	6.5	2.4	0.8	2.2	79.4	12.7	3.8	0.7	3.4
2000	84.8	5.4	1.8	0.7	7.3	80.4	12.4	1.9	0.8	4.4
2002	86.8	5.2	5.8	0.8	1.4	80.6	12.1	5.4	0.6	1.3
2005	83.2	5.3	9.1	1.1	1.4	81.6	11.7	5.5	0.4	0.8
2006	84.5	4.7	8.5	1.0	1.4	82.9	10.5	5.4	0.4	0.8

Source: Bank of Korea: Monthly Statistical Bulletin.
Note: Trade in services is not included.
ª DM represents the euro starting from 2000.

Asian countries not trading with Japan but with each other—as when Thailand trades with Malaysia—everything is typically invoiced in dollars. Even Japanese trade with other East Asian countries is invoiced more in dollars than in yen. Outside of Europe, the prevalence of dollar invoicing is also true in other parts of the world. For example, in Latin America, exports are largely dollar invoiced, and intraregional trade is entirely dollar invoiced.

For manufactures, more than pure invoicing is involved. Exporters everywhere outside of Europe typically opt to quote selling prices for their products in dollars, and then keep these dollar prices fairly constant in industrial catalogs and other published price lists. In effect, they price to the world market—and not just to the American one—in dollar terms. Thus national central banks aiming to stabilize the international purchasing power of their currencies, often opt—either formally or informally—to peg against the dollar, and thus against the huge sticky-priced mass of internationally traded goods that it represents.

Fourth, if we think of a *standard of deferred payment*—which is also a traditional role of money—private and sovereign bonds in international markets are heavily denominated in U.S. dollars, though the euro did seem to be as important. Table 2.6 is difficult to interpret because "international" also refers to intra-European issues of euro-denominated bonds. But this ambiguity aside, the growth of a broadly based euro-denominated bond market within Europe made it much more attractive for foreigners to borrow by issuing euro bonds or "deposit" by buying euro-denominated bonds. So the euro area with its previously strong currency was unusual in being a gross creditor in the world economy, that is, being able to lend in its own currency.

However, because of the recent crisis of the euro, table 2.6 shows a precipitate drop in international bond issues in euros—from 42.4 percent in 2009 to just 19.6 percent in 2010—a downward trend probably accentuated in 2011. By contrast, table 2.6

Table 2.6. NET INTERNATIONAL ISSUES OF DEBT INSTRUMENTS
(PERCENTAGE OF TOTAL ISSUE)

By currency of issue

	Dollar	Euro zone currencies and euro*	Pound	All other currencies	Memorandum: Net issues in $billion
1998	60.3	33.0	8.4	−1.8	**681**
1999	44.4	47.7	7.1	0.8	**1,230**
2000	50.1	37.8	8.4	3.7	**1,234**
2001	48.4	44.3	5.2	2.1	**1,348**
2002	41.5	51.7	6.2	0.6	**1,429**
2003	31.5	56.9	6.8	4.8	**1,463.9**
2004	25.1	58.3	9.3	7.3	**1,614.2**
2005	25.9	54.3	12.4	7.4	**1,860.9**
2006	40.5	44.9	8.6	6.0	**2,773.1**
2007	42.5	41.6	7.9	8.0	**3,002.6**
2008	28.4	42.6	25.1	3.9	**2,430.7**
2009	49.8	42.4	7.5	0.3	**2,335.7**
2010	74.4	19.6	3.3	2.7	**1,506.7**

By nationality of issuer

	United States	Euro zone countries	United Kingdom	Other industrial countries	Developing countries and offshore centers	International institutions
1998	41.1	31.4	7.7	4.0	7.6	8.2
1999	39.2	41.3	9.4	3.9	4.2	2.2
2000	37.7	45.0	9.7	0.9	4.9	108
2001	44.3	40.9	5.7	2.7	5.2	1.2
2002	32.6	47.4	9.9	3.6	4.4	2.1
2003	18.4	52.5	14.5	7.3	5.7	1.6
2004	14.6	49.3	14.7	13.9	6.1	1.4
2005	14.8	51.0	15.8	9.8	6.9	1.8
2006	28.1	42.8	14.1	8.6	6.0	0.4
2007	34.2	37.6	10.8	10.2	6.0	1.3
2008	23.6	38.1	26.4	8.2	1.3	2.3
2009	25.9	39.5	11.2	12.4	6.6	4.4
2010	35.3	25.8	6.0	11.7	15.0	6.2

Source: Bank for International Settlements.

shows that dollar-denominated bond issues rose sharply from 49.8 percent in 2009 to 74.4 percent in 2010. This "flight to safety" in dollars is one indication of the remarkable resilience of the dollar standard in crisis times.

Emerging markets, such as China with trade surpluses, are more or less confined to lending in dollars, that is, accumulating liquid dollar bonds or illiquid other assets arising out of direct investment abroad. If developing countries have cumulative trade deficits, they cover them by borrowing in dollars. U.S. Treasuries are still taken as the benchmark or "risk-free" asset in international bond markets. That is, dollar-denominated sovereign bonds issued by emerging markets the world over have their credit ratings (by Moody's, Standard and Poor's, or Fitch) measured relative to U.S. Treasuries. Thus, risk premia in interest rates on these bonds are typically quoted as so many percentage points over U.S. Treasuries.

In summary, the use of the dollar in facilitating international commerce in goods or in financial assets is still surprisingly ubiquitous despite the great financial traumas emanating from the United States—to which the world has been subject over the last four decades—which we will describe further in chapter 4.

NOTES

1. True, transacting in dollars can encroach on the natural domains of domestic currencies. Such "dollarization" occurs when the domestic currency has become very unattractive because of a history of high inflation, such as in Zimbabwe or Ecuador, where households use dollars to buy their groceries. But, for the most part, dollarization in domestic trade is rare if only because governments mandate that the domestic money be legal tender. But no such legal tender constraint exists for international money changing.

2. Making predictions based on current trends, Arvind Subramanian (2011) in his book *Eclipse* projects that by 2030 China will account for more than 23 percent of world GDP and America less than 12 percent at purchasing power parity exchange rates. These projections may or may not turn out to be accurate, but they don't undermine the argument presented here that dollar-based exchange will continue to increase as world trade grows with GDPs.

CHAPTER 3

⌒

The Dollar as a Worldwide Nominal Anchor

Insular U.S. Monetary Policy from 1945 to the Late 1960s

From 1945 through most of the 1960s, reconciliation of America's international and domestic monetary objectives was not a problem. The lack of confidence in the currencies of Europe and Japan, whose industrial and financial sectors had been flattened by the war, leading to open and repressed inflation, meant that they had to ring-fence their economies with exchange controls to prevent capital flight. Early in this era was the "great dollar shortage": people and corporations wanted to hold mainly dollar assets with their unique international liquidity. This natural role of the dollar as the key currency in the postwar monetary order was simply "legalized" by the 1945 Bretton Woods Agreement.

The implosion of the international gold standard in the 1920s and 1930s had generated "hot" money flows that led to "beggar-thy-neighbor" exchange rate policies and the Great Depression. The victorious allies—led by the United States and Britain—resolved never again to allow large exchange rate fluctuations or uncontrolled financial flows across currency boundaries. In this brave new international monetary order, gold was dethroned as the common monetary anchor and the dollar was enthroned. Outside the United States, countries declared fixed dollar exchange parities that could be changed only moderately and with the permission of the newly created International Monetary Fund. Outside the foreign exchange markets, other *governments* could sell U.S. Treasury bonds for gold to the U.S. government at $35 per ounce.

By 1945, the United States had accumulated almost all the world's gold. People at the time did not project that the U.S. gold obligation would be anything more than pro forma, and would not constrain American policy. Thus the United States alone as the Nth country at the center of the Bretton Woods monetary order was free to determine its own monetary policy and price-level objective. In contrast, other countries had to subordinate, at least in part, their domestic monetary policies to maintain their dollar exchange parities. This asymmetrical system worked well as long as the U.S. federal government (1) successfully stabi-lized its own (and hence the world's) price level in dollars, and (2) did not object to how other countries set their exchange rates against the dollar.

When Western European countries began to recover under the Marshall Plan, they did so by fixing their exchange rates firmly against the dollar. The capstone of the Marshall Plan was the formation of the European Payments Union (EPU) in July 1950. Sixteen Western European countries declared exact dollar parities (without even small margins around these central rates) at which only their *central banks* cleared intra-European payments multilaterally while incidentally anchoring their price levels. (Open private foreign exchange trading was not yet permitted.) In parallel, with the help of an American line of dollar credit known as the Dodge Line, Japan eventually managed to stabilize its macroeconomy by choosing 360 yen to the dollar in 1949 as the anchor for phasing out inflation and restoring a modicum of confidence in the yen (McKinnon and Ohno 1997).

With the important exception of West Germany, industrial countries other than the United States maintained capital controls well into the 1970s. With the fully convertible dollar as the clearing currency, the Western European countries and Japan had adopted more limited current-account convertibility by the early 1960s. Together, these monetary structures were sufficient to promote explosive growth in multilateral trade: the engine of extraordinary economic growth from 1950 into the early 1970s.

COMECON: AN ASIDE ON CURRENCY INCONVERTIBILITY

From 1945 through the 1980s, the large communist bloc— including China, the Soviet Union, and Eastern Europe—had currencies that were not even convertible on current account. In organizing voluntary trade between nations within the bloc, their own currencies—which had differing (disequilibrium) national prices—were totally unusable. In the event, the dollar was used as a unit of account to price out the "value" of each communist country's putative export basket to a designated bloc neighbor.

How did this work in practice? In the late 1940s, the Soviets set up a bureaucracy, the Council for Mutual Economic Assistance (COMECON) that hosted member countries once a year to negotiate the exchange of baskets of tradable goods within each pair of communist countries. COMECON'S job was to prepare *dollar* price lists of all relevant goods—primary commodities from, say, the Chicago Board of Trade or manufactures from, say, German industrial catalogs. Then a negotiating team from each communist country could value its desired export basket at international relative prices. Even so, when, say, Poland traded with Bulgaria, the particular items to be traded were subject to heated bilateral bargaining—although their aggregate values traded bilaterally would turn out to be about equal in dollar terms.

However, for ideological reasons, the dollar was not used as a means of settlement within COMECON. Thus multilateral trade within the bloc was next to impossible. Trade between any pair of communist countries was narrowly balanced bilaterally through barter-type negotiations with no net capital flows. Within the bloc, the last thing any negotiator wanted was to run a trade surplus and be forced to acquire the deficit-country's inconvertible currency in exchange (McKinnon 1979, ch. 3).

THE WORLD'S PRICE LEVEL

The American wholesale price index (WPI) approximates a worldwide index of tradable goods' prices reinforced by the practice of dollar invoicing of so much of world trade. Figure 3.1 shows the U.S. WPI to be remarkably stable from the 1950s into the late 1960s during the Bretton Woods period of fixed dollar parities. However, figure 3.1 also shows how, after 1970, this anchoring stability was lost with the breakdown of the Bretton Woods fixed dollar parities; figure 3.2 shows the yen and the deutsche mark beginning to appreciate against the dollar.

But more than just the stability in the American price level was lost. Before 1970, with fixed dollar exchange rate parities, the WPIs of major trading partners such as Germany and Japan, with convertible currencies on current account, closely tracked the stable American WPI as shown in figure 3.3—as did those of a host of smaller economies (not shown). In effect, the industrial countries had a common price level for tradable goods.

Then with the breakdown of the fixed parity regime after 1970 and advent of inflation in the United States, the WPIs of Germany and Japan inflated less quickly—and diverged from the American level as well as from each other. The benign effect on investment efficiency of having a common "world" price level in the 1950s and 1960s was lost. And indeed productivity growth in the industrial countries slumped sharply in the 1970s into the 1980s

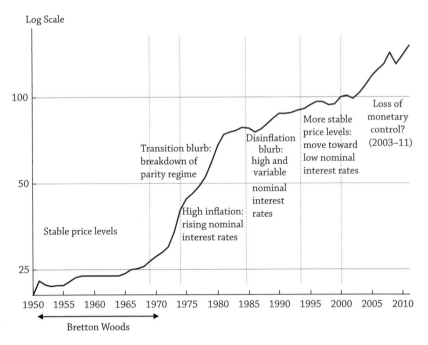

Figure 3.1.
The World's Nominal Anchor: U.S. Wholesale Prices (1951–2011)
Source: www.bls.gov

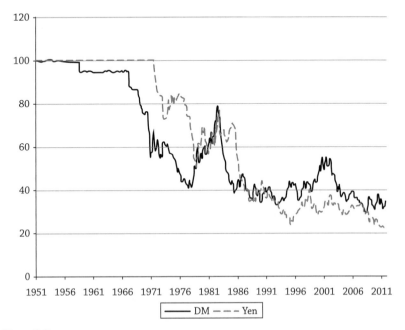

Figure 3.2.
U.S. Nominal Exchange Rates (1951–2011)
Source: Bundesbank, www.globalfinancialdata.com

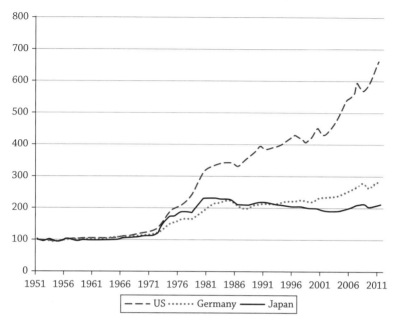

Figure 3.3.
Wholesale Price Indices
Source: Statistisches Bundesamt Deutschland, www.globalfinancialdata.com

with large exchange rate fluctuations and highly variable inflation rates.

This early dominance of the dollar in determining national price levels until 1970 was unintended. Under the Bretton Woods Agreement of 1945, national monetary autonomy was supposed to be paramount. Because of the disastrous collapse of the international gold standard in the interwar period, J. M. Keynes in particular was adamant that never again should national monetary and fiscal policies be subordinated to an international standard. But the intentions of the authors of international monetary treaties are not necessarily borne out in practice. After the war, more by necessity than design, the stable dollar became the monetary anchor for most national price levels outside the communist bloc (McKinnon 1979).

During the early postwar period of highly successful noninflationary growth, there were many controversies—particularly between monetarists and Keynesians—on how U.S.

monetary policy should be conducted. But the foreign exchanges were left out of both sides of the debate. The protagonists treated the American economy as if it was closed. But luckily the lack of substitutability between dollars and the currencies of the other industrial economies with exchange controls before 1970 meant that the Fed could conduct an inward-looking monetary policy relatively successfully. It could ignore the ebb and flow of the demand for dollars in the foreign exchanges and focus just on conditions in the huge American economy, such as employment and inflation—while benignly neglecting the rest of the world.

These rather special historical circumstances of the early dollar standard conditioned the American monetary authorities to become *insular*. They concluded that the demand for money (dollars), and various operating rules governing Federal Reserve behavior, could be based on purely domestic financial indicators such as U.S. inflation and unemployment, or the reserve positions of American commercial banks with the Fed. And this inward-looking U.S. monetary policy turned out to be correct for the time.

Unfortunately, this insular view became enshrined in U.S. textbooks on money and banking, and on monetary policy more generally, long after financial globalization and the shrinkage in the relative size of the American economy had made it obsolete. In particular, this insularity has carried over to today's era when runs from dollars into foreign currencies—and vice versa—have become commonplace (ch. 5). By ignoring the information contained in these runs, the Fed has become much less effective in stabilizing the domestic American financial system and price level, while undermining the anchoring function that the dollar had provided to the rest of the world—as shown in figure 3.3.

How this (international) instability was generated after 1970 and its consequences is the theme of chapters 4 and 5 to follow. But first let us consider the effect of the unique American obligation under the IMF's Article IV to buy or sell at $35 per ounce. Did this constrain American policy in the 1950s and 1960s?

THE DOLLAR-GOLD EXCHANGE STANDARD (1959–68)

Despite all the EPU's great advantages in reestablishing a monetary basis based on the dollar for intra-European trade in the 1950s, it had certain economic limitations:

1. Intra-European payments were placed on substantially different basis than trade with non-European countries. The latter had to be financed by open market purchases and sales of foreign exchange. The clearing machinery of the EPU permitted discrimination against purchases of goods from outside the union—particularly the United States itself!
2. The EPU relied heavily on national central banks for clearing all settlements. Indeed this funneling of transactions through central banks facilitated the maintenance of exchange controls and payments restrictions to outsiders.

Hence, on December 24, 1958, the European Payments Union was officially disbanded, and exchange restrictions against dollar area imports were removed. Fourteen Western European countries—including all the industrial ones—made their currencies fully externally convertible for current transactions under Article VIII of the 1945 Bretton Woods Agreement, and also made fully operational the par-value obligation under Article IV as then stated:

1. The par value of the currency of each member shall be expressed in terms of gold as a common denominator or in terms of the United States dollar of the weight and fineness in effect on July 1, 1944.

2. The maximum and minimum rates...shall not differ from
   parity...in the case of spot exchange transactions by more
   than one percent. (Horsefield 1969, 189)

As a practical matter, it was awkward to buy and sell gold directly
for fiat currencies in the open market in order to maintain exchange
margins. Gold is costly to store and transport, and the world gold
supply was still in the late 1950s asymmetrically concentrated in
the United States. Moreover, European countries had already been
maintaining exact dollar parities as part of the EPU agreement.
Thus, in 1959, Article IV was interpreted such that member countries of the IMF all pegged their currencies to the U.S. dollar within
a 1 percent margin on either side of parity. Each national central
bank kept reserves to buy or sell dollars for the domestic currency
in the open market for foreign exchanges in order to maintain the
2 percent band width for all who wished to trade with the country
in question. Thus the dollar became the *official intervention currency*
used by European and other central banks the world over.[1]

Most importantly, in this brave new world of the dollar-gold
exchange standard, responsibility for clearing international
payments when exchange rates were within the 2 percent band
(which was most of the time) devolved away from central banks
to commercial banks authorized to deal in the interbank market
for foreign exchange. (Investment banks, such as Goldman Sachs
and Morgan Stanley, had not yet made an appearance in this
role—although they have huge foreign exchange trading desks
today.) To acquire foreign exchange for, say, 90 days hence, a nonbank importer could contract with its local commercial bank to
buy the foreign exchange forward. If necessary, the local bank
could then cover itself by purchasing the forward foreign exchange
in the interbank market. Unlike the old EPU, central banks need
not be directly involved in clearing international payments or
making a forward market.

What were the reciprocal American obligations in the brave
new monetary order? The formal obligation under Article IV was

to fix the dollar's parity in terms of gold. While all other countries pegged dollar, the American authorities agreed to sell (or buy) gold to foreign central banks upon demand in exchange for U.S. Treasury bonds at a fixed parity of US $35 per ounce with no band of variation. Such government-to-government transfers took place outside the open market for foreign exchange. Thus, the world was put on a full-fledged dollar-gold exchange standard.

The second important American obligation under the dollar-gold exchange standard was implicit. Because all foreign central banks were intervening with their own currencies to maintain their 1 percent bands against the dollar, the U.S. Federal Reserve Bank essentially stayed out of the open foreign exchange markets in order to avoid conflict.[2] The Bank of England, for example, would buy or sell dollars for sterling to maintain the exchange rate between US$2.78 and US$2.82, but the Federal Reserve Bank would stay out of the dollar-sterling market—and also stay out of a hundred or so other markets in foreign currencies. Indeed, the United States didn't, and still doesn't, hold significant reserves of other currencies with which to intervene. And this American passivity in allowing other countries to choose their exchange rates against the dollar was, and still is, an essential element in the harmonious working of the global monetary system. (The analytical details of this asymmetrical system were developed in chapter 2.)

An important consequence, however, was that the American government did not have direct control over the state of its balance of payments in the 1960s—nor should it have then or now. As long as other countries set their exchange parities and interest rates at desired levels vis-à-vis the dollar so they had overall payments surpluses, they could accumulate as many U.S. dollar bank accounts and Treasury bonds as they wanted. The net American balance of payments was simply a residual.

But American authorities responded with alarm to the resulting accounting "deficits" in American foreign payments, even when America was running large trade surpluses in the early

1960s. In fact, the capital outflow from the United States—including direct investment and purchases of longer-term foreign bonds—was greater than the U.S. trade surplus. The difference was a short-term capital inflow.

Instead of welcoming the voluntary buildup of dollar reserves by foreigners in a period of worldwide price stability, in the 1960s the American authorities saw such foreign accumulation as an indirect threat to the American gold reserves—and tried (without success) to restrict some kinds of capital outflows from the United States.

As partial *quid pro quo*, however, the United States could use its own dollars to cover payments "deficits" as they developed, whereas other countries had to use scarce foreign exchange. Influential French economists have called this asymmetry an "exorbitant privilege of the United States" indicating that official misinterpretations of international monetary phenomena were not confined to the American side of the Atlantic.

Before discussing the reasons for the inevitable collapse of the pure dollar-gold exchange standard, let us describe its rather remarkable accomplishments. For the industrial economies, it allowed free multilateral exchange of their convertible currencies among private commercial banks and trading firms without having to channel foreign payments through central banks. Within the 1 percent margins on either side of the parity, exchange rates were very stable and payments restrictions on current account transacting were absent so that domestic monies in the industrial economies were virtually as good as international money. Meanwhile, under GATT, tariffs—and particularly quota restrictions—on commodity trade among the industrial countries were more easily reduced when exchange rates were stable. Foreign trade grew even more rapidly than national incomes in the 1960s, so that all the industrial economies became more open to foreign trade, as output per capita rose impressively by any historical standard.

(It should be noted that most less developed countries maintained inconvertible currencies in the 1950s and 1960s, and also maintained payments restrictions as well as tariff and quota bar-riers on imports. This import-substitution strategy of economic development meant, effectively, that most did not participate in the postwar world trade boom and their economies became more closed. Indeed, we have a paradox. U.S. aid in the late 1950s and 1960s to less developed countries was often associated with more centralized planning [India, Latin America] and the imposition of restraints on foreign trade, whereas the earlier, more success-ful Marshall Plan aid to Europe was associated with the removal of trade restrictions! Quite possibly, the Agency for International Development administrators in the 1950s and 1960s failed to recognize the monetary reasons for the Marshall plan's success.)

Stability in a macroeconomic sense was also achieved. Those countries that effectively fixed their exchange parities to the U.S. dollar, and kept convertible currencies on current account, had their price levels (in terms of tradable goods) pegged to those in the United States—the latter being quite stable from 1951 to the mid-1960s, as indicated in figure 3.3.[3] Their domestic monetary policies had to be adjusted to maintain this fixed exchange rate, while accommodating quite high rates of growth in real output. Indeed, a convincing peg to the U.S. dollar allowed Germany and Japan, which had experienced traumatic monetary upheavals in the late 1940s, to restore confidence in the deutsche mark and yen faster than would otherwise have been the case. Inflationary expectations were also dampened elsewhere in Europe if citizens came to believe that their government was committed to a fixed dollar parity. (This earlier favorable experience induced many countries to continue their dollar parities into the early 1970s, well past the point that it was desirable to do so.)

THE UNITED STATES AS BANKER TO THE WORLD

A truly international capital market was an outgrowth of the dollar-gold exchange standard, and essential to its smooth functioning. Countries and individuals who were net savers (surplus units in a financial sense) could deposit in New York banks or buy bonds in New York, whereas countries that had a need for investment resources (deficit units in a financial sense) could borrow in New York, with both creditors and debtors using the dollar as a vehicle currency. And in the late 1950s and 1960s, New York with its offshoot "euro" dollar market in London was the dominant entrepôt for international capital, although not on the grand scale that London had been prior to 1914 under the gold standard with sterling being the vehicle currency. Still America came close to being the world's banker.

Besides bringing net savers and investors together, financial intermediation through the dollar had another important aspect. Governments abroad had a continuous need to tailor their own reserves of freely usable dollars for intervention or precautionary purposes, and commercial banks also had a demand for dollar checking accounts and term deposits because of the dollar's role as a vehicle currency. Either group was then free to borrow at long term—say, by issuing bonds—in New York, and use the proceeds to build up its short-term liquidity: freely usable dollar deposits in New York or London.[4] This freedom to borrow long and lend back (deposit) short in dollars did not result in any *net* international transfer of capital. Yet foreigners could acquire international liquidity when they needed it, and hence more easily preserve currency convertibility with fixed rate exchange rates.

Notice that it was not necessary for the United States to actually run a current-account deficit (as it does now) to supply the rest of the world with international liquidity. As long as U.S. capital outflows, much of which were illiquid direct investment in overseas factories or mines, exceeded its current-account surplus, the return flow in the balance of payments was the buildup of dollar bank accounts and Treasury bonds owned by foreigners providing international liquidity.

THE TRIFFIN DILEMMA

In discussing the collapse of the dollar-gold exchange standard and fixed exchange rates, I shall first look at the proximate reasons for virtually ending, in 1968, American gold sales to foreigners—and then discuss the deeper reasons rooted in the increasing instability of the American economy in the late 1960s.

After the European recovery, the world's stock of monetary gold changed little: the official price was fixed at $35 per ounce until 1971, and the net flow of newly mined gold for industrial use was small relative to existing monetary stocks (see table 3.1). In 1951, the total official gold reserves of IMF members amounted to $33.5 billion and were $38.7 billion in 1968. Of this, official American holdings amounted to $22.9 billion in 1951, but fell to $10.9 billion by 1968. Rapidly growing European economies allowed their dollar reserve positions to grow commensurately mainly by purchasing dollars in the open markets for foreign

Table 3.1. OFFICIAL GOLD HOLDINGS AND EXTERNAL DOLLAR LIABILITIES OF THE UNITED STATES (BILLIONS OF DOLLARS)

Year	Official world gold holdings	Official U.S. gold stocks*	Outstanding dollar claims on U.S. held by foreign banks
1951	33.5	22.9	8.9
1956	35.7	22.1	15.3
1960	37.7	17.8	21.0
1964	40.5	15.4	29.4
1968	38.7	10.9	38.5
Closing of the American gold window			
1972	38.5	10.5	82.9
1974	43.3	11.8	119.1
1976	41.3	11.2	144.7

Source: *International Financial Statistics* (various issues).
Note: Gold is evaluated at official dollar prices through time. After 1968, the open-market price for gold was two or three times this official price. Nevertheless, no major country could sell all of its official gold in the open market without driving the price down quite drastically. Therefore, choosing a correct price for evaluation is difficult.

exchange to maintain their dollar parities. However, some—particularly the French—chose to convert their dollars into gold, which the U.S. Treasury was obligated to supply at $35 per ounce.

More frightening to American authorities was the rapidly rising stock of dollar claims on the United States held by foreign banks (commercial and central) that had not yet been converted. These rose from about $8.9 billion in 1951 to $38.5 billion in 1968, as shown in table 3.1. Thus claims potentially convertible into gold in 1968 amounted to more than three and a half times the remaining American gold, thus posing the Triffin Dilemma (Triffin 1960):

> How did this affect American decision making? Concern with protecting the last American gold reserves and avoiding the inevitable run on the bank prompted the American authorities in the mid-1960s and afterwards to pressure friendly governments not to convert existing dollar holdings, as was their right under Article IV. Finally, on March 15, 1968, official sales of gold by a consortium of central banks (including the United States Federal Reserve System) on the open private gold market in London were terminated, thus segmenting the official price of gold from the free market price. And subsequently the free-market price has fluctuated well above the official price of $35 per ounce, which was raised to $42 in 1971. Although the American gold window was not closed officially by President Nixon until August 1971, negligible American sales of gold to foreign central banks took place after 1968.

Worse than simply leaning on foreign central banks not to convert dollars into gold was the spate of balance-of-payments restrictions on capital outflows imposed by Presidents Kennedy and Johnson: (1) the interest-equalization tax on foreign securities sold in the United States in 1963, (2) the restrictions on bank lending to foreigners in 1965, and (3) attempts to force multinational corporations in 1968 to finance their foreign operations overseas. These were concrete responses to accounting balance-of-payments "deficits"—the overseas buildup of dollar claims on the United States (see table 3.1)—that in turn augmented official fears of losing gold. If effective, such restraints would have seriously impeded the key role of the New York capital market in providing dollar liquidity to the rest of the world. Fortunately, these regulatory efforts were undercut by the development of the Eurodollar market centered in London, outside the web of American capital controls.[5] Hence, an international capital market continued to provide dollar liquidity as well as bringing net savers and investors together. And the American balance-of-payments restrictions themselves were eventually terminated in 1974.

From table 3.1, the buildup of official dollar reserves by foreign central banks as the world economy grew were potential dollar claims on the American gold stock—and sooner or later would force termination of the U.S. Treasury's unlimited obligation to convert extant dollars into gold. Balance-of-payments restrictions seeking to limit lending to foreigners contributed to the market's nervousness and were ultimately self-defeating.[6] But America's principal international monetary obligation under the de facto international dollar standard was not the pro forma link to gold but rather to maintain stable dollar prices of internationally tradable goods as well as an open capital market. This it did successfully throughout the 1950s and into the mid-1960s (see figure 3.1).

However, inflationary pressure developed in the United States in the late 1960s from failing to finance properly the Vietnam War and President Johnson's parallel expansion of the American welfare state. Wholesale prices began to increase moderately at 3 to 4 percent per year. Having to accept even this modest inflation upset major inflation-phobic trading partners, such as West Germany. In addition, with fixed dollar exchange parities, it also upset American industrialists who felt that they were losing international competitiveness. But faced with the choice between disinflating or devaluing the dollar, the American government chose dollar devaluation: the "Nixon shock" to be discussed in chapter 4 that ultimately cracked the system of fixed exchange rates. The harmonization of stable monetary policies across the world's major industrial economies came to an end—although the dollar's role as a facilitator of international trade remained.

WAS THE GOLD TIE A CONSTRAINT ON AMERICAN MONETARY POLICY?

Robert Triffin taught us that the American obligation to convert dollars into gold at $35 per ounce under the IMF's Article IV would eventually have to be abrogated as the world economy grew and official dollar exchange reserves grew relative to monetary gold stocks. But a deeper and more difficult question to answer still is whether the "good" American monetary behavior, that is, stable wholesale prices in the 1950s on into the late 1960s, was conditioned by this gold tie.

Put differently, if gold had been entirely phased out of the dollar-based system, that is, demonetized with the U.S. Treasury being neither a buyer or seller, as eminent authors such as Emile Despres (1965) wanted, would the now unconstrained American monetary policy have been so stable?

In my early incarnation as a young man (McKinnon 1969, "The Case for the Dollar as International Money") I believed that the demonetization of gold was the right way to go. "In a world of recurrent crises in the gold and foreign exchange markets, it is all too easy to forget the great progress that has been made under the dollar-based system. Rapid growth in world trade in goods and securities has been enormous by any historical standard. These crises should not obscure the fact that a little adroit tinkering with the system can permit growth to continue even faster without the crises. Completing the demonetization of gold, correcting one or two exchange rates that are badly out of line, and removing American restrictions on outflows of capital while keeping stable domestic prices would be sufficient. It would be tragic if recurrent crises were to inculcate the psychology of an inevitable collapse in the dollar standard. There are no handy alternatives" (McKinnon 1969, 34).

Clearly I badly misjudged the ongoing inflationary pressure in the United States from government policy influenced by the Phillips Curve Fallacy on the one hand, and the Exchange Rate and Trade Balance Fallacy on the other—as described in chapter 1. But this will become clearer as chapters 4 and 5 unfold.

NOTES

1. An ever-decreasing number of former British colonies continued to fix their exchange rates in terms of sterling, and a similar overseas franc area was maintained in Africa among former French colonies. Canada floated without an official par value from 1950 to 1962. Otherwise, virtually all other members of the IMF did define their exchange parities in dollars.
2. Among LDCs parities were frequently changed. Notice that it is sufficient to establish *all* the cross rates of exchange in the system if each country intervenes against a common intervention currency, e.g., the U.S. dollar.
3. Of course, countries suffering from often massive internal inflations—such as Argentina, Brazil, Chile—could maintain neither fixed parities nor convertible currencies.
4. This process is described in more analytical depth in Kindleberger 1965.
5. A more complete description of the fascinating financial phenomena of Eurocurrency trading can be found in McKinnon 1979, ch. 9.
6. Britain managed the pre-1914 gold standard with even more slender gold reserves behind extant sterling claims. But everyone realized that the Bank of England would undertake a contractionary monetary policy to defend itself against gold losses—unlike the Federal Reserve System in the 1960s.

CHAPTER 4

✦

The Slipping Anchor, 1971–2008

The Nixon, Carter, and Greenspan Shocks

The dollar has become increasingly unsatisfactory as an anchor for price levels and financial stability in the American and world economies. How can this be measured?

First consider the long-term purchasing power of the dollar in a comparative international context. Figure 4.1 plots the path of the U.S. and German CPIs since 1957, when comparable data first became available, and then splices the CPI for the euro area in 2010 onto the German series through 2010. When the euro area is spliced in, its inflation rate is very similar to that of Germany's—past and present. Since 1957 inflation in the United States has averaged 4 percent, while Germany's (and the euro area's) is close to 2.7 percent. Because many central banks around the world ostensibly target annual CPI inflation to be about 2 percent, the German-led continental Western Europeans clearly have provided better long-term price-level stability despite the euro's recent travails.

What about the short and medium terms? Much of the erratic behavior of American monetary policy in the medium term can be captured by plotting the exchange rate of the dollar against the more stable mark-euro (again spliced together as of 1999) as shown

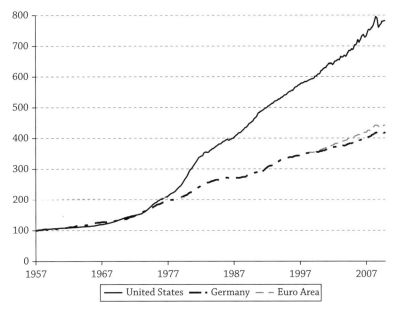

Figure 4.1.
Consumer Price Indexes for the United States, Germany, and the Euro Area
Source: IFS and globalfinancialdata.com

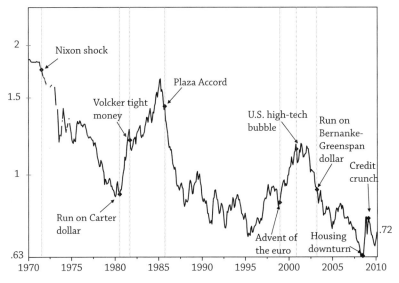

Figure 4.2.
Mark-Euro/USD Exchange rate, 1950–2010
Note: Exchange rates before 1999 are calculated with DM rates.
Source: www.globalfinancialdata.com and Federal Reserve Economic Data

in figure 4.2. When the dollar was weak and falling (sometimes because the U.S. government "talked" it down), this triggered a flight of hot money from the United States, and a fall in the demand for money in the United States itself. In each episode, the falling dollar fomented worldwide inflation in commodity and/or asset prices that eventually rebounded on the United States. As suggested by figure 4.2, the outstanding examples of this syndrome of a falling dollar were the Nixon shock in 1971–73, carrying over to the Carter shock in 1977–78, and the Bernanke-Greenspan shock in 2003–04. (The more purely Bernanke shock of 2008–12 is analyzed in chapter 5.) Consider each in turn.

THE NIXON SHOCK LEADING TO WORLD INFLATION IN THE 1970S

In the late 1960s, under pressure from financing the Vietnam War and pressure from domestic social expenditures, mild inflation began in the United States (figure 3.1). Because of the fixed dollar exchange parities from the Bretton Woods Agreement, U.S. industry became less competitive against that of most other industrial economies. However, instead of disinflating by raising interest rates to restore U.S. international competitiveness, the American government chose to maintain monetary ease while insisting that the other industrial countries all appreciate their currencies against the dollar. This was the famous Nixon shock of August 1971. Indeed, Nixon imposed a tariff on manufactured imports entering the United States and threatened to keep it on until the Western industrial economies appreciated substantially, which they all did between 10 and 20 percent—as ratified by the so-called Smithsonian Agreement in December 1971. (Japan appreciated by 17 percent.)

Because heated public discussion of possible dollar devaluation had already begun by 1970, hot money began flooding out of U.S. dollars into all the European currencies and the yen *before* actual dollar depreciation in 1971. This flight from the dollar resulted in a fall in the demand for money in the United States with no offsetting reduction in supply. Combined with a lower dollar in the foreign exchanges, the stage was set for the great U.S. inflation of the 1970s.

Surprisingly, this loss of monetary control was first evident in the industrial economies on the dollar standard's periphery and not in the United States itself. Figure 4.3 shows the smooth growth in U.S. M1 from 1970 to 1981 of about 2 percent per year despite wide fluctuations in the dollar's effective exchange rate and wild bouts of inflation in U.S. price indexes—the CPI in figure 4.4 and WPI in figure 4.6. Having the U.S. M1 growing smoothly at about 2 percent per year seems inconsistent with a monetary explanation of the great inflationary swings of the 1970s.

Then as now, the key to understanding the impact of unstable monetary-cum–exchange rate policies in the United States is to look first at their monetary consequences in relevant countries on the dollar standard's periphery. By 1970, the relevant periphery was the industrial countries of Western Europe, Canada, and Japan—whose economic recoveries and currency convertibility put them into the "hard" money category. (In 2012, the most relevant

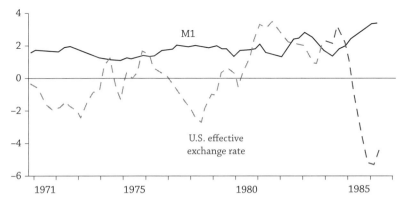

Figure 4.3.
Rate of Change in U.S. Money Supply (M1) and in Effective Dollar Exchange Rate, 1970–86
Source: McKinnon 1996

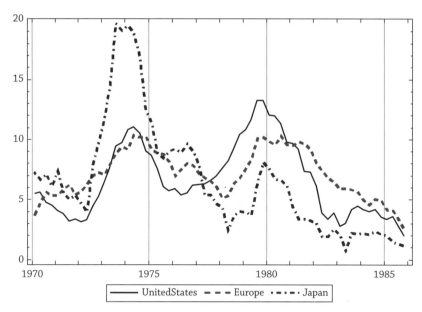

Figure 4.4.
Consumer Price Index of the Principal Western European Countries, United States, and Japan
Source: globalfinancialdata.com

periphery has become major emerging markets with high growth and high "natural" rates of interest—as discussed in chapter 5.)

What was the inflation transition mechanism from center to periphery and then back again? Because of doubts about future U.S. monetary policy and commitment to future exchange rate stability, hot money continued to flow out of the United States even after the supposed one-time Nixon dollar depreciation ratified in the Smithsonian Agreement of December 1971. Other countries, industrial and some developing, tried to resist further appreciations against the dollar beyond what had been agreed to with President Nixon. Each central bank intervened to buy dollars to prevent its national currency from appreciating precipitately against its neighbors. But collectively this triggered a general explosion in their dollar foreign exchange reserves. Table 4.1 shows the foreign exchange reserves of Japan, Western Europe, and Canada, surging about 60 percent per year in 1970–72. Because they could not fully sterilize the monetary consequences

Table 4.1. DIRECT DOLLAR LIABILITIES OF THE U.S. TO FOREIGN CENTRAL
BANKS AND GOVERNMENTS (BILLION DOLLARS, YEAR-END STOCKS)

Year	Canada	Japan	Western Europe	Total	Annual percentage change
1970	2.95	3.19	13.61	19.75	**74.8**
1971	3.98	13.78	30.13	47.89	**142.5**
1972	4.25	16.48	34.20	54.93	14.7
1973	3.85	10.20	45.76	59.81	8.9
1974	3.66	11.35	44.33	59.34	−0.8
1975	3.13	10.63	45.70	59.46	0.2
1976	3.41	13.88	45.88	63.17	6.2
1977	2.33	20.13	70.75	93.21	**47.6**
1978	2.49	28.90	93.09	124.48	**33.5**
1979	1.90	16.36	85.60	103.86	**−16.6**
1980	1.56	21.56	81.59	104.71	**0.8**
1981	2.40	24.72	65.22	92.34	**−11.8**
1982	2.08	19.17	60.72	81.97	**−11.2**
1983, Q3	2.76	20.45	63.25	86.46	5.5

Source: McKinnon 1996.

of buying dollars with domestic base money, their national money supplies also surged in 1970–73. Figure 4.5 shows the sharp increase in "ROW" (rest of the world) money in the form of M1 in 1970–72 (McKinnon 1982).

Inflation became high in both Europe and Japan despite the appreciations of their currencies against the world's central money. Figure 4.4 shows the surge in inflation in the CPIs of the Western European counties, Japan, and the United States from 1973 to 1975, and figure 4.6 shows the even higher surge in their PPIs (producer price indexes). Primary commodity prices including oil also rose sharply from the worldwide inflationary pressure.

But notice that monetary control in these periphery countries was lost (figure 4.5) well before the first oil shock. The Yom Kippur War, followed by an Arab embargo on world oil supplies, started in September 1973. Undoubtedly, the sudden supply constraint on Middle East crude coming onto the market would have caused the price of oil to jump. But the inflationary genie had already

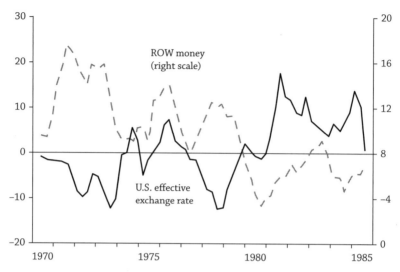

Figure 4.5.
Rate of Change in Effective Dollar Exchange Rate and in Rest of the World (ROW) Money,
1970–86
Source: McKinnon 1996

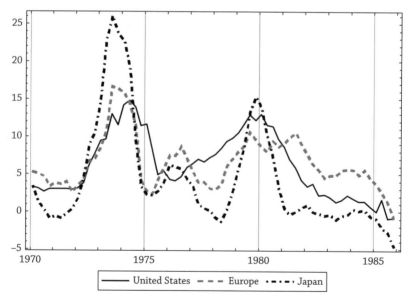

Figure 4.6.
Producer Price Indexes of the Principal Western European Countries, United States, and
Japan
Source: globalfinancialdata.com

been let out of the bottle because of the flight from the dollar starting in 1970 and the huge increase ROW money in 1971–72. So the size of the jump in the price of oil in 1973–74, if attributed only to the supply constraint, surprised even the most militant Arab sheiks.

THE CARTER SHOCK OF THE LATE 1970S

The sharp global recession of 1975–76 damped the ongoing worldwide inflation temporarily (figures 4.4 and 4.6). But the incoming administration of U.S. President Jimmy Carter was also fixated on "unfair" foreign mercantile competition, and his advisers were heavily in thrall to the Exchange Rate Cum Trade Balance Fallacy. (By then, high inflation combined with high unemployment had weaned many people off the Phillips Curve Fallacy.) At the end of 1976, the Carter government embarked on another campaign to depreciate the dollar—particularly against the yen. Despite his doubts, Secretary of the Treasury Michael Blumenthal was dragooned into giving speeches suggesting that the dollar should be lower and the yen higher. In 1977–78, the result again was another run of hot money out of the United States, another surge in dollar foreign exchange reserves (table 4.1), excessive money growth abroad in 1977–78 (figure 4.5), and a second burst of worldwide inflation (figures 4.4 and 4.6).

Finally, in October 1978, an international consortium of the major industrial countries rescued the dollar from further declines with actual and threatened intervention to support it. Part of the agreement was a sharp increase in U.S. interest rates to halt further outflows of hot money—and the package did succeed in putting a floor under the dollar.

Note that the Iranian revolution, and second big disruption in world oil supplies, did not occur until 1979—well *after* the run on the Carter dollar. So the surge in dollar exchange reserves (table 4.1) and loss of monetary control in peripheral industrial

countries (figure 4.5) had already occurred in 1977–78. The inflation genie of excessive money issue had been let out of the bottle
before the advent of hostilities in Iran and sharp increases in oil
prices in 1979–80.

In retrospect, these disruptions in the marketing of oil
provided, and still provide, a deceptive cover for the two great
inflationary episodes of the 1970s. Most people just remember
them as "oil shocks" that caused the great inflations. But the
worldwide loss of monetary control, following the Nixon shock
of 1971 and then the Carter shock of 1976, both leading to a
depreciating dollar, was the primary engine of inflation in both
cases. In large part, the surprisingly sharp increases in the price
of oil (figure 4.7) were largely endogenous to the preceding surges
in money growth in Western Europe and Japan.

True, there is an identification problem. How much of the two
great surges in the price of oil in 1973–74 and again in 1979–80
(figure 4.7) can be attributed to a prior loss of monetary control
from a malfunctioning dollar standard, and how much from the

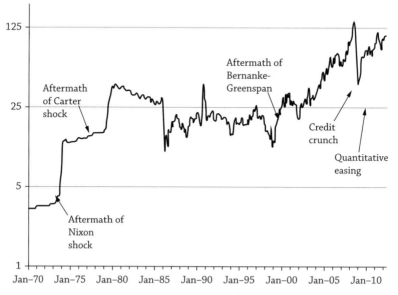

Figure 4.7.
West Texas Intermediate Oil Price, 1970–2010
Source: globalfinancialdata.com

sudden supply constraints in the form of embargoes by major exporters? Fortunately, a "natural" experiment suggests itself to help sort things out.

The world suffered another big shock when the price of oil more than tripled between 2002 and July 2008 (figure 4.7). But this time, there were no obvious politically based disruptions in the supply of oil. As will be discussed more comprehensively in chapter 5, this last oil shock can again be attributed to hot money out-flows from the United States because of unduly low interest rates in 2003–06, leading to a weak and falling dollar. But this time the relevant periphery was (is) large emerging markets—China, India, Brazil, Russia, and Indonesia—whose central banks intervened heavily to buy dollars But in most people's minds, the great infla-tions of the 1970s are dimly remembered as "supply side" oil shocks rather than as worldwide monetary shocks arising out of a malfunctioning world dollar standard—as hypothesized here.

High and variable inflations with wild exchange fluctuations continued into the 1980s until the new Fed chairman, Paul Volcker, ended the inflation with an extremely tight money policy in 1981–83. Short-term interest rates rose to more than 20 per-cent in 1981 so that the dollar shot up in the foreign exchanges (figure 4.2), resulting in a sharp decline in U.S. manufacturing in 1982–84, the advent of the so-called rust bowl, largely in the American Midwest. This international monetary turmoil knocked the industrial economies off their paths of high, noninflationary productivity growth—which had prevailed under stable exchange rates and monetary stability of the 1950s and 1960s. The general slowdown in productivity growth in the 1970s and early 1980s was much greater than could be explained by "exogenous" oil shocks.

In light of these disasters, one might ask why the U.S. government failed to disinflate in the late 1960s when inflation was still quite mild (3 to 4 percent per year) compared to what was to come in the 1970s (figures 3.1 and 3.3)—and thus pre-serve the dollar's anchoring effect for the rest of the world. The short answer is that the U.S. government—like most others in the 1960s—was in thrall to the Phillips Curve Fallacy: the trade-off between inflation and unemployment. It imagined that by tolerating (slightly) higher inflation the economy would settle down to a permanently lower rate of unemployment. Thanks to Milton Friedman (1968), and to actual experience with high inflation coupled with high unemployment in the in the 1970s, this fallacy has been discredited. Doctrinally, we are now in somewhat better shape to reestablish an international monetary regime with stable exchange rates. But the exchange rate–cum–trade balance fallacy is still alive and well, and undermines reestablishing a strong dollar as an anchor for the world price level.

THE BERNANKE-GREENSPAN SHOCK AND THE BUBBLE ECONOMY, 2003–08

Fast-forward 20 years to consider a more recent episode of a persistent fall in the foreign exchange value of the dollar, again using the euro for comparison. Figure 4.2 shows the dollar falling persistently from about 1.2 euros in 2002 (the top of the U.S. high-tech bubble) to about 0.63 euro in July 2008—when U.S. interest rates averaged much less than European ones. This unduly easy U.S. monetary policy did not show up as high inflation in the U.S. core CPI (figure 4.8), which excludes more volatile items such as food and energy. By focusing on inflation in the U.S. core CPI, which showed a modest 2 percent or so annual inflation in this purely domestic (and backward-looking) price-level indicator, the Fed missed the bubbles in asset prices in both the American and world economies. Figure 4.8, courtesy of Steve Hanke (2010), shows that the Commodity Reserve Bureau (CRB) index, a very of broad index of dollar commodity prices, rose more than 90 percent from the first quarter of 2003 to peak out in the second quarter of 2008. The price of oil (figure 4.7) rose even more sharply than the general commodity price indexes.

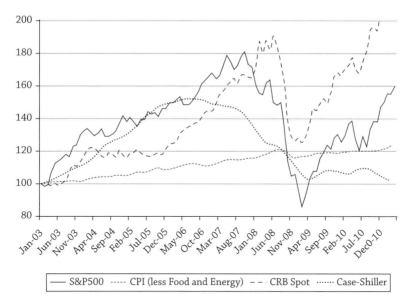

Figure 4.8.
The Greenspan-Bernanke Bubble Economy, 2003–10
Source: Bloomberg and Federal Reserve Economic Data

Housing prices, measured by the Case-Schiller index, surged 44.7 percent from the first quarter of 2003 to their peak in the first quarter of 2006.

Why did the Fed actively stoke these bubbles? Fearing deflation after the collapse of the high-tech bubble in 2001–02, the U.S. Federal Reserve Bank lowered the Fed funds interest rate to just 1 percent in 2003–04. At the time, this interest rate was far too low for balancing actual inflation in the "headline" CPI with the economy's excess capacity. The well-known Taylor Rule suggested that the Fed funds rate should have been closer to 4 percent in 2003–4 (Taylor 2009).

Beyond the Taylor Rule violation, however, the persistent weakness of the dollar from 2002 to mid-2008 should have also signaled to the insular Fed that American monetary policy was far too loose. The asset bubbles themselves were not the only indicator. Large emerging markets (EMs) with naturally higher interest rates and floating exchange rates, such as Brazil, were particularly discomfited by the sharp appreciations of their currencies and loss of internal monetary control. China, which was trying to maintain a more stable dollar peg, also experienced hot money inflows that made control of its monetary base increasingly difficult. The People's Bank of China had to undertake massive sterilization efforts to mop up excess monetary liquidity that was contributing to the bubble in commodity prices, and then to reimpose controls on capital inflows. But the Fed, with its orientation toward only domestic monetary indicators, ignored all this.

This insular view of how *American monetary policy* should be conducted interacted with another major economic fallacy: the so-called efficient markets theory. Although observers in the Federal Reserve and elsewhere could see the extraordinary increases in asset prices from 2002 into 2008 shown in figures 4.7 and 4.8, they chose to ignore them. The prevailing doctrine of efficient markets convinced the Fed that such bubbles would be efficiently self-correcting without any countervailing action by the central bank.

In summary, the Fed's insularity regarding events in the international economy, particularly the falling dollar and associated bubbles in asset prices, combined with the Efficient Markets Fallacy on the one hand and the Exchange Rate and Trade Balance Fallacy on the other (a lower dollar will reduce the trade deficit) culminated in the bubble economy—whose bursting led to the subprime mortgage crisis and great credit crunch of 2008–09. In effect, the Fed overreacted to the bursting of the dot-com bubble in 2001 by reducing interest rates too much, and seems to have overreacted again to the subprime mortgage bust by setting short-term interest rate near zero after December 2008—as we shall see in chapter 5.

CHAPTER 5

⤲⤲

The Bernanke Shock, 2008–12

Interest Differentials, Carry Trades, and Hot Money Flows

WHAT DOES *CURRENCY CARRY TRADE* MEAN?

It is a strategy in which an investor sells a certain currency with a relatively low interest rate (the funding currency) and uses the funds to *purchase* a different currency yielding a higher interest rate (the investment currency). A trader using this strategy attempts to capture the difference between the rates, which can often be substantial, depending on the amount of leverage used. The big risk in a carry trade is the uncertainty of exchange rates. The carry trader would run the risk of losing money if the investment currency suddenly depreciates but would gain further if it appreciates. Also, these transactions are generally done with a lot of leverage, so a small movement in exchange rates can result in huge losses unless the position is hedged appropriately.

This Wikipedia description is useful but not complete. A key feature of a carry trade is that the trader does not (cannot) hedge his position against foreign exchange risk. From covered interest arbitrage, we have the well-known result that the interest differential i (funding) minus i^* (investment) approximately equals the forward premium $f = (F - S) / S$, where F is the forward, and S the spot exchange rate: investment currency / funding currency. So if the trader sells the investment currency forward to cover himself, the preexistence of covered interest arbitrage exactly wipes out his profit because $f = i - i^*$. To get back into the funding currency, the cost of forward cover, that is, the forward premium f, is equal to the interest differential. Carry trading is a risky business where hedging is virtually useless!

CARRY TRADING FROM THE FED'S ZERO-INTEREST-RATE POLICY

From 2009 into mid-2011, almost all emerging markets (EMs) complained about ultralow interest rates at the "center" inducing hot money flows to the "periphery." With the two-speed world recovery, the slowly growing mature industrial countries—the United States, Europe, and Japan—have cut short-term interest rates very low. Figure 5.1 shows short-term interbank interest rates in the United States to be near zero since the end of 2008: the Bernanke shock. This is then followed by declines in short rates on euros (Germany) and the pound sterling to less than 1 percent by mid-2009 and continuing into 2012. Japan had been stuck in a zero-interest liquidity trap since the mid-1990s.

In addition, the U.S. Federal Reserve's Quantitative Easing (QE) for reducing long rates (ending in June 2011) exacerbated the problem. Figure 5.2 shows the 10-year bond rate in the United States, U.K., and the euro area (Germany) approaching 2 percent in 2011, with the 10-year bond rate of Japan down to just 1 percent. No wonder carry traders get excited with the prospect of

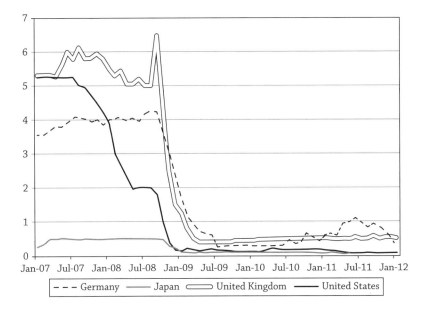

Figure 5.1.
Post-crisis Money Market Interest Rate of the Developed World
Source: Global Financial Data

much higher interest rates in emerging markets on the dollar standard's periphery.

The long swing in the American portion of the current carry trade began in 2002. After the dot com bubble burst in 2001, the Fed (over)reacted by cutting the U.S. interbank interest rate to just 1 percent from 2002 into 2004—and then raised it very slowly despite economic recovery and the advent of bubbles in housing prices and in worldwide commodity markets. The resulting carry trade induced a flood of hot money into emerging markets—which have higher growth and naturally higher interest rates. The result was a steadily depreciating dollar on a trade-weighted basis until 2008, as shown in figure 5.3. This more or less steady dollar depreciation (appreciation in emerging markets) magnified the short-term profits of carry traders in the 2002–08 period.

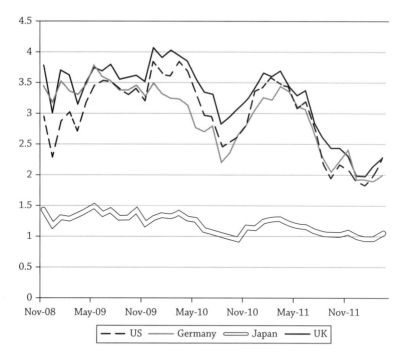

Figure 5.2.
10-Year Government Bond Rate of Selected Countries (November 2008 to March 2012)
Source: IMF

However, this seemingly lucrative carry trade was interrupted by the worldwide bank credit crunch from the last half of 2008 into 2009. The crisis demand for dollars shot upward, and figure 5.3 shows the dollar rising sharply in the foreign exchanges. Highly leveraged dollar carry traders were caught by banks suddenly refusing to roll over their short-term loans in dollars. The traders were forced to sell off their foreign exchange assets to repay their dollar loans, whence the sharp rise in the dollar in the foreign exchanges in 2008 (figure 5.3).

Because the United States has had near-zero short-term interest rates from late 2008 onward, the stage was set for the revival of the carry trade once the credit crunch was over. Indeed, once banks resumed their "normal" lending to carry traders, the dollar began to weaken again from early 2009 to mid-2011 (figure 5.3), and the relaxation of bank credit also induced another

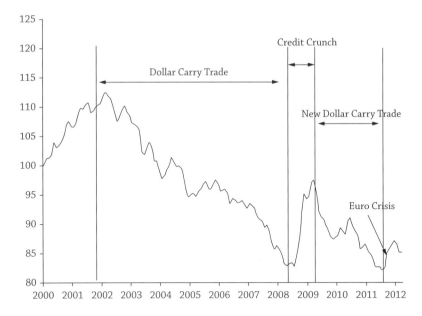

Figure 5.3.
The Nominal Broad Dollar Index Movements (January 2002 = 100)
Source: Federal Reserve Economic Data

"mini" surge in commodity prices from 2009 to mid-2011, as shown in figure 5.4.

But then another surprise came. The "exogenous" crisis in Europe over the fate of Greece and the euro became a full-fledged worldwide banking crisis by the summer of 2011. Bank credit seized up from counterparty risk over European sovereign debt uncertainty among the banks themselves. Again carry traders were caught on the hop as normal bank credit was cut off. They had to sell off their foreign exchange assets and long positions in commodities. In the fall of 2011, the dollar rose somewhat in foreign exchanges (figure 5.3), while commodity prices began to fall (figure 5.4). The upshot is that a weakening dollar from carry trading goes hand in hand with surging commodity prices, as reflected in a longer-term perspective in figure 4.8 on the Greenspan-Bernanke bubble economy. Clearly, allowing wide interest differentials to persist between the center and periphery is a recipe for chronic macroeconomic instability.

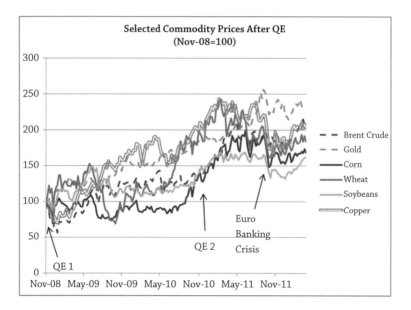

Figure 5.4.
Selected Commodity Prices after QE (November 2008 = 100)
Source: Global Financial Data

THE PLIGHT OF EMERGING MARKETS

For emerging markets only, figure 5.5 is the mirror image of figure 5.3, and shows their ongoing nominal appreciation since 2002, as the counterpart of the dollar's slow depreciation. Figure 5.6 shows that China's modest appreciation from 2002 to early 2011 cumulated to be about the same as other emerging markets—but the upward course of the RMB has been smoother and more predictable.

So the combination of very low American interest rates and a declining dollar has provoked large outflows of financial capital ("hot" money) into EMs for almost a decade. When EM exchange rates are not tied down by official parities, their endogenous ongoing appreciation induces even more hot money inflows. Trend-following (chartist) carry traders see a double benefit: the higher EM interest rates combined with their currencies appreciating against the dollar or yen. For 2000–07 before the global credit crunch in 2008, table 5.1 provides illustrative returns to

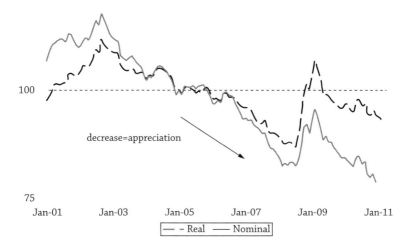

Figure 5.5.
EM Percentage Nominal Exchange Rate Appreciation (January 2005 = 100)
Source: Haver Analytics, Morgan Stanley Research
Emerging markets (EMs) include the following countries: Russia, Poland, Czech Republic, Hungary, Romania, Ukraine, Turkey, Israel, UAE, Saudi Arabia, South Africa, China, India, Hong Kong, Korea, Taiwan, Singapore, Indonesia, Malaysia, Thailand, Brazil, Mexico, Chile, Peru, Colombia, Argentina, Venezuela

Table 5.1. RETURNS ON CARRY TRADE (2000–07)

Funding currency	Interest rates		Returns from appreciation	Returns of carry trades	Investment currencies
	Funding	Investment			
U.S. dollar	3.4	10.2	1.1	7.9	Brazil, Mexico, and Canada
Euro	3.2	7.4	1.0	5.2	Iceland, Poland, and Czech Republic
Japanese yen	0.1	5.3	5.2	10.7	Australia, Korea, and New Zealand

Source: IMF

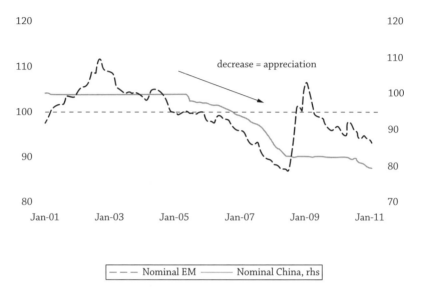

EM and CHN Nominal Exchange Rate Appreciation, Jan'05=100

Figure 5.6.
EM and China Nominal Exchange Rate Appreciation (January 2005 = 100)
Source: Haver Analytics, Morgan Stanley Research

borrowing in dollars, euros, or yen to invest in surrounding EMs. The annual returns to dollar-based carry traders investing in Brazil, Mexico, and Canada were about 7.9 percent.

For emerging markets, therefore, exchange rate flexibility is no protection from foreign interest rate disturbances—as when the Fed reduces its short rates to zero. In the short run, exchange rate flexibility may actually enhance the returns that carry traders see as the target EM investment currency appreciates against the dollar. To slow the appreciations of EM currencies, EM central banks typically intervene to buy dollars with domestic base money. And these interventions have been truly massive. Figure 5.7 shows that from the first quarter of 2001 to the first quarter of 2011, the dollar value of EM foreign exchange reserves rose sixfold—from $1 trillion to $7 trillion! Figure 5.7 also shows that China accounted for about half of this huge buildup—but the collectivity of other EMs was equally important.

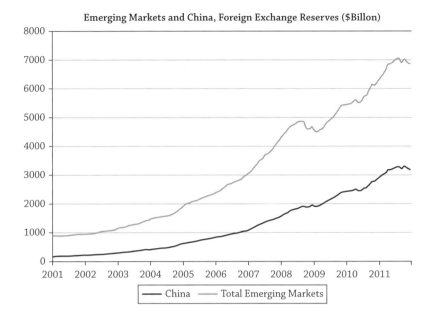

Figure 5.7.
Emerging Markets and China, Foreign Exchange Reserves ($Billion)
Source: IFS
Emerging markets (EMs) include the following countries: Russia, Poland, Czech Republic, Hungary, Romania, Ukraine, Turkey, Israel, UAE, Saudi Arabia, South Africa, China, India, Hong Kong, Korea, Singapore, Indonesia, Malaysia, Thailand, Brazil, Mexico, Chile, Peru, Colombia, Argentina, Venezuela. Data missing for UAE from October 2011 and for Venezuela at December 2011, approximated by previous periods

Figure 5.8 shows that this EM buildup of foreign exchange reserves increased much faster than the growth of their nominal GDPs. For the EM group, reserves rose from about 15 percent of GDP at the beginning of 2001 to 34 percent of GDP at the beginning of 2011. Figure 5.8 shows that for China alone over this same 10-year period, the ratio of foreign exchange reserves to GDP increased particularly strongly, from 13 to 50 percent. Some EMs, notably China and Brazil, have reimposed exchange controls on capital *inflows*—but with limited success.

This sharp buildup of EM foreign exchange reserves has been too big to be fully offset by domestic monetary sterilization operations. The resulting loss of monetary control in the EMs led (and leads) to inflation generally higher than that in the developed market economies (DMs)—as shown in figure 5.9. This greater inflation in EMs

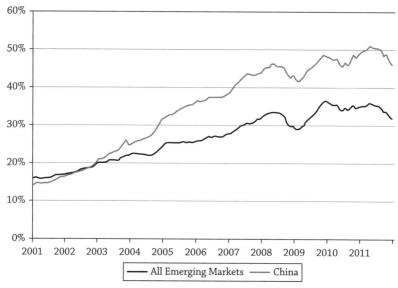

Figure 5.8.

Emerging Markets and China, FS Reserve-GDP Ratio

Source: IFS

Notes: Calculated from annual GDP. Assume constant intrayear growth rate. Months in 2011 use 2010 GDP growth rate

Emerging markets (EMs) include the following countries: Russia, Poland, Czech Republic, Hungary, Romania, Ukraine, Turkey, Israel, UAE, Saudi Arabia, South Africa, China, India, Hong Kong, Korea, Singapore, Indonesia, Malaysia, Thailand, Brazil, Mexico, Chile, Peru, Colombia, Argentina, Venezuela. Data missing for UAE from October 2011 and for Venezuela at December 2011, approximated by previous periods

occurred *despite* the fact that, since 2002, EM currencies on average appreciated against the DM currencies, as shown in figure 5.5.

More recently, after the interruption of the 2008 global credit crunch, a renewed carry trade began and was led by the now zero short-term interest rates in the United States. Table 5.2 shows from May 2009 into mid-2011 the continued rapid buildup of foreign exchange reserves in the largest EMs—China, Russia, Indonesia, India, and Brazil—all of which have nominal CPIs growing more than 5 percent per year. This is substantially higher than CPI or PPI inflation in Europe or Japan, or in the United States itself. China's ongoing trade surplus (without any normal offsetting capital outflow) also contributes to its buildup of foreign exchange reserves—but is no longer dominant.

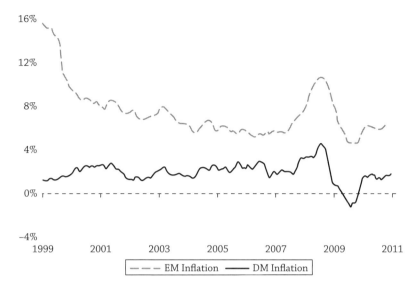

Figure 5.9.
Emerging Market (EM) and Developed Markets (DM) Inflations
Source: Haver Analytics, Morgan Stanley Research
Developed markets (DMs) include the following countries: United States, Germany, France, Italy, Spain,
Japan, United Kingdom, Canada, Sweden, Australia

Stephen Green of Standard Chartered Bank shows (figure 5.10) that net financial inflows into China in the last quarter of 2010 and first quarter of 2011were much bigger than its trade surplus. And Green estimates that in the first quarter of 2011 China's foreign exchange reserves rose by $152 billion even though its trade surplus was negligible. Hot money inflows, then, seemed to be the main source of China's increased foreign exchange reserves before the euro banking crisis—as they were in the first half of 2008 (figure 5.8) before the global credit crunch took hold in the second half.

On a world scale, the most striking inflationary impulse is seen in primary commodity prices. Year-over-year to June 21, 2011, *The Economist*'s dollar commodity price index for all items shows an average increase of 38.6 percent, with food prices alone rising 39 percent. For the past decade, figure 4.8 gives a longer perspective on various asset price bubbles—including two extraordinary surges in commodity prices before and after the global credit crunch of 2008.

Table 5.2. FOREIGN EXCHANGE RESERVES (BILLION DOLLARS)

	Brazil	China, mainland	India	Indonesia	Russian Federation
May-09	194	2,093	253	56	387
June-09	200	2,135	255	55	396
July-09	206	2,178	262	55	385
August-09	215	2,224	267	58	392
September-09	221	2,288	271	60	395
October-09	230	2,344	273	62	414
November-09	235	2,405	270	63	425
December-09	237	2,416	265	64	417
January-10	239	2,432	263	67	414
February-10	240	2,441	260	67	413
March-10	243	2,464	261	69	423
April-10	246	2,507	261	76	436
May-10	249	2,456	255	72	429
June-10	252	2,471	256	73	433
July-10	256	2,556	266	76	448
August-10	260	2,565	263	78	447
September-10	274	2,667	272	83	458
October-10	283	2,780	276	89	464
November-10	284	2,786	270	90	449
December-10	287	2,866	275	93	444
January-11	296	2,952	278	92	451
February-11	306	3,012	280	96	458
March-11	316	3,067	283	102	465
April-11	326	3,168	290	110	483
May-11	331	3,188	288	113	480
Percentage increase from May 2009	71%	52%	14%	102%	24%

Source: IFS

Near-zero interest rates in the mature industrial countries contribute to commodity price inflation in two ways. First, they generate hot money inflows into the emerging market periphery—as analyzed here—and EM demand for primary commodities rises. Second, once commodity prices begin to rise, commodity carry traders find they can borrow ultra cheaply in New York or Tokyo to fund long positions in commodity futures. Of course,

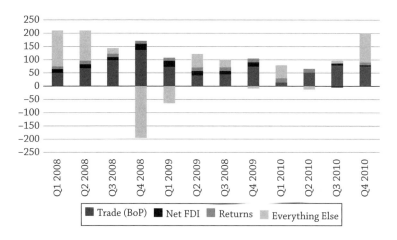

Figure 5.10.
Components of China's Foreign Exchange Reserve Growth
Source: Standard Chartered

this adds to the upward price *momentum* making commodity prices, and asset prices in general, more prone to bubbles—as a glance at figure 4.8, The Greenspan-Bernanke Bubble Economy, would suggest.

But also notice from figure 4.8 that the U.S. core CPI index, which excludes food and energy prices, has yet to register any of this inflationary pressure. This backward-looking index, which includes the post-bubble downward fall in house prices and rents, is the Fed's favorite inflation target! With the Fed looking the other way, this international inflation will eventually—albeit with a lag of somewhat uncertain duration—come back to the United States and other mature industrial countries, perhaps in the form of the "stagflation" reminiscent of the 1970s.

(This analysis was written before the second big international banking crisis, beginning about August 2011, from the implosion of confidence in the euro. This second banking crisis then cut off bank credits to carry traders, interrupted hot money flows, and suddenly relieved the inflationary pressure on peripheral countries. Whether this interruption is temporary or not remains to be seen—but I will return to it chapter 13).

CARRY TRADES AND INTERNATIONAL
MONETARY REFORM

What are the implications for international monetary reform? In the new millennium, I have argued, world monetary instability has been (and is) provoked by large and persistent interest differentials that induce carry trades: the willingness of speculators to borrow in low-interest-rate currencies (source currencies) to invest in higher-yield currencies (investment currencies). But what can governments do about this?

One of the principal designers of Bretton Woods, J. M. Keynes, was adamant that capital controls be retained to minimize cross-currency financial flows. Keynes wanted the new system to be insulated from the hot money flows characteristic of the 1920s and 1930s, which had undermined, and then caused, the implosion of the interwar gold standard leading to worldwide depression. Instead, Keynes wanted *national macroeconomic autonomy* (McKinnon 1993), where each nation remained free to set its own interest rates and conduct its own fiscal policy to secure full employment without being bound by an international standard. So, to this day, under the IMF Articles of Agreement, any signatory is free to impose exchange restrictions on capital account. Although doing so is legal for all countries, the United States itself could not possibly impose capital controls. Because the dollar is the key currency, the whole system of clearing international payments multilaterally would collapse.

From 1945 to the late 1960s, most industrial countries and virtually all developing ones kept capital controls in place. But unlike what Keynes wanted or projected, a common international monetary standard was reestablished. The stable-valued dollar became the common anchor for keeping national price levels roughly aligned, as discussed in chapter 3, and the need for dramatically different interest rates was minimal. Although imperfect, the old system of fixed dollar parities eliminated the possibility of prolonged exchange rate movements in one direction, on which carry traders now thrive.

Compared to the 1950s and 1960s, today's worldwide carry-trade problem has become more acute because exchange rates are more flexible and because of the relaxation of controls on international movements of financial capital—at least in part at the misguided behest of the IMF as a necessary step toward economic "liberalization." (However, illiquid longer-term direct foreign investments are not a problem.) Fortunately, over the last two years, the IMF now seems to have reversed itself and is more tolerant of controls on liquid international capital flows—but only after a lot damage had been done.

The Asian crisis of 1997–98 was worsened by an earlier carry trade with Japan. By 1995, Japan had fallen into a near-zero interest rate liquidity trap with a weakening yen. Hot money poured out of Japan and into the Asian Crisis Five: Indonesia, Korea, Malaysia, Philippines, and Thailand. Although Japan was not the only source for overborrowing by the Crisis Five, they became badly overextended in their foreign-currency indebtedness. Thus when speculators attacked Thailand in June 1997, the contagion spread to the other four by the end of the year—with capital flight, widespread financial bankruptcies, sharp exchange rate depreciations, and sharp downturns in output and employment. Japan was hurt as its exports to other East Asian countries slumped. Fortunately, China ignored foreign advice to depreciate the renminbi in tandem. Instead, the yuan/dollar rate was kept stable—which made it easier for its five smaller East Asian trading partners (and competitors) and Japan to recover.

Today, the carry-trade story is no better. The prolonged dollar depreciation after 2002 (figure 5.3) with ultralow U.S. interest rates led to the huge buildup of foreign exchange reserves (figure 5.7) in the EMs. Similarly over the last decade, misdirected pressure on China to continually appreciate the RMB has given carry traders a one-way bet on foreign exchange movements that they really love. Notice that this explanation differs from the common view (Rajan 2010, 82) that Asian countries were so badly burned by the 1997–98 crisis that they turned conservative and resolved to run large trade surpluses to build up their foreign reserve positions. But today's large Asian official exchange reserves are far in excess of any such prudential motivation and much larger than their cumulative trade surpluses.

How best can carry trades be limited? Central bankers from the G-20 major economies could meet continually to monitor each other in order to prevent wide interest differentials from developing. True to its newly professed virtue, the IMF should refrain from criticizing countries that attempt to impose capital controls to stem hot money flows. It could also provide technical advice on how to do so most efficiently.

But if interest spreads are too wide, capital controls will always fail. The first item on the G-20 agenda should be to abandon monetary policies by the mature economies that set interest rates near zero, which encourages emerging markets to keep their interest rates low despite the inflationary pressure they now face. The Fed must be the leader in raising interest rates because, under the asymmetrical world dollar standard, it has the greatest autonomy in monetary policy.

But American officials point to the stagnant U.S. economy as the reason they want to keep domestic interest rates as low as possible—even zero. Thus, they have to be convinced that this common view is mistaken, and that raising short-term interest rates on dollar assets from zero to modest levels is in America's own best interests—as well as those of the rest of the world.

THE SUPPLY CONSTRAINT ON BANK CREDIT

How do near-zero interest rates in U.S. interbank markets constrict the American economy? Since July 2008, the stock of base money in the U.S. banking system has virtually tripled. As part of its rescue mission in the crisis and to drive interest rates down and flood markets with liquidity, the Fed has bought many nontraditional assets (mortgage-backed securities) as well as Treasuries. However, these drastic actions have not stimulated new bank lending. As shown in figure 5.11, much of this huge increase in base money is now lodged as excess reserves (cash assets) in large American commercial banks: a *liquidity trap.* In addition, figure 5.11 shows that banks have invested heavily in Treasury and Agency securities.

Despite the Fed's strenuous efforts, the supply of ordinary bank credit to firms and households remains weak. Figure 5.11 shows outstanding Commercial and Industrial Loans falling from $1.62 trillion in October 2008 to just $1.30 trillion in October 2011. Although large corporate enterprises have recovered from the credit crunch of 2008 through their renewed access to bond and equity financing, bank credit is the principal source of finance for working capital for small and medium-sized enterprises (SMEs), enabling them to purchase labor and other

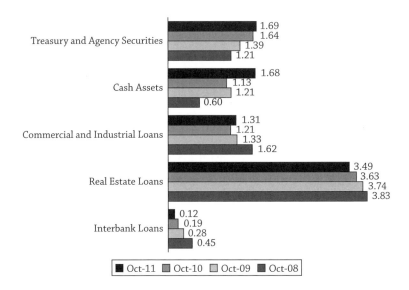

Figure 5.11.
Holdings of Bank Assets at Commercial Banks in the United States ($trillion)
Source: Federal Reserve Economic Data

supplies. In cyclical upswings, SMEs have traditionally been the main engines for increasing employment. But in the very weak upswing of 2009–11, employment gains have been meager or nonexistent.

Why should zero-interest rates be causing a credit constraint? After all, conventional thinking has it that the lower the interest rate the better credit can expand. But this is only true when interest rates—particularly interbank interest rates—are comfortably above zero. Banks with good retail lending opportunities typically lend by opening credit lines to nonbank customers. But these credit lines are open-ended in the sense that the commercial borrower can choose when—and by how much—he will actually draw on his credit line (subject to some maximum limit of course). This creates uncertainty for the bank in not knowing what its future cash positions will be. An illiquid bank could be in trouble if its customers simultaneously decided to draw down their credit lines.

However, if the "retail" bank has easy access to the "wholesale" interbank market, its liquidity is much improved. To cover unexpected liquidity shortfalls, it can borrow from banks with excess reserves with few or no credit checks. But if the prevailing interbank lending rate is close to zero (as it is now), then large banks with surplus reserves become loath to part with them for a derisory yield. Then smaller banks, which collectively are the biggest lenders to SMEs, cannot easily bid for funds at an interest rate significantly above the prevailing interbank rate without inadvertently signaling that they might be in trouble, that is, distress borrowers. And indeed counterparty risk in smaller banks remains substantial, as almost 100 failed in 2011. (Remember that the huge Fed and TARP bailouts of 2008–09 were limited to large banks deemed too big to fail.)

That the American system of bank intermediation is essentially broken is reflected in the sharp fall in interbank lending: Figure 5.11 shows that interbank loans outstanding in October 2011 were only slightly more than one-quarter of their level in October

2008, just after the crisis hit. How to fix bank intermediation and escape from the liquidity trap is a long story (McKinnon 2009 and 2010a). However, raising short-term interest rates above zero is an important part of the story.

But the damage that near-zero interest rates have done to financial intermediation in the United States is more general than that seen just in banking statistics. Money market mutual funds attract depositors who believe they can withdraw their deposits to get virtually instant liquidity. But as the yields on the short-term liquid assets of these funds approach zero, a small negative shock could cause any of them to "break the buck" if marked to market. That is, a customer trying to withdraw from his account might get only 99 cents on the dollar. Banks and other sponsors of money market mutual funds are paranoid about the reputational risks of breaking the buck. So they have closed, or are closing, money market mutual funds both in Europe (in euros) and in the United States (in dollars).

Although expanding bank and mutual fund credit to nonfinancial firms is important enough, the United States should also raise interest rates moderately to prevent pension funds from going bust in the medium term. With short-term interest rates so close to zero and Fed chairman Ben Bernanke pledging to keep them there until the economy improves (perhaps as late as 2014), this must drive down long rates. Remember that long rates today reflect the path of expected short rates into the future plus a liquidity premium. And figure 5.2 shows that the American 10-year bond rate on Treasuries is already down to just 2 percent.

In California, public pension plans have typically assumed yields of about 7.5 percent on their assets to meet their fixed pension obligations. Clearly, in today's interest rate environment, they can't do it even if they were "fully" funded by the 7.5 percent criterion. Private life insurance companies are also very stressed in meeting their annuity obligations to policyholders. And these financial intermediaries have been important sources of long-term finance for American industry. So, in its own domestic interest, the United States itself desperately needs to get interest rates up from rock-bottom levels—and needs to curb the carry trades that are so upsetting internationally.

A CONCLUDING NOTE ON STAGFLATION IN THE UNITED STATES

The Fed's zero-interest-rate policy has worsened the situation and made escape to a more normal flow of bank intermediation more difficult. Without more lending to SMEs, domestic economic stagnation will continue even though inflation will take off.

The stagflation of the 1970s was brought on by unduly easy U.S. monetary policy in conjunction with attempts to "talk" the dollar down (the Nixon shock of August 1971), leading to massive outflows of hot money that destabilized the monetary systems of America's trading partners (McKinnon 1982) and generated worldwide inflation (ch. 4). Although today's stagflation is not identical, the similarities would seem to be more important than the differences.

Today's "shock" is the Fed's overreaction to the global downturn of 2008 by setting the short-term federal funds rate close to zero. So the solution is more straightforward. The Fed should announce a program for gradually increasing the Fed funds rate to some modest target, say 2 percent. This should be accompanied by a definite program for reducing the counterparty risk in interbank lending to all banks but particularly small ones, possibly by allowing them to pledge loans to SMEs as collateral.

To better preserve financial and exchange rate stability in the transition, the big four central banks—Fed, European Central Bank, Bank of England, and Bank of Japan—should move jointly and smoothly to phase in a common minimum target—say 2 percent—for their basic short-term interbank rates while relaxing any commitment they may have made to keep long rates down indefinitely. By escaping from liquidity traps that so impair the efficiency of domestic bank intermediation and aggravate the international bubbles problem, the mature center itself would benefit along with its periphery.

Reducing the spread in interest rates between the center and periphery would dampen carry trades and hot money flows in an important way. But it may not be sufficient to end them altogether. So acknowledging the legitimacy of emerging markets using capital controls and other devices to dampen hot money inflows should be an important part of the new G-20 discussion. Indeed central banks in the mature center could monitor their own commercial banks to help central banks on the periphery enforce their controls.

(But there is an important asymmetry here. Capital controls are not for everybody. In particular, the United States at the center of the world dollar standard cannot itself impose capital controls without destroying the world's system for clearing international payments multilaterally. Thus everybody has a vested interest in rehabilitating the unloved dollar standard with open U.S. financial markets. The first of many necessary steps in the rehabilitation process is for the Fed to abandon any thought of a QE3 while phasing out its policy of keeping short rates near zero.)

These cyclical carry trades illustrate the main point of the chapter: wide interest rate differentials across currencies make the world monetary system much more fragile whatever the exchange rate regime. "Reform" efforts should focus much more on international monetary harmonization that limits interest differentials while accepting the need for exchange rate buffers, such as capital controls, to limit hot money flows. Once the European banking crisis recedes (if ever), the large interest differential—near-zero interest rates in the United States and much higher natural interest rates in the high-growth EMs—will set off another cycle of hot money flows from the center to the periphery.

PART TWO

Trade Imbalances

CHAPTER 6

⌇

The U.S. Saving Deficiency, Current-Account Deficits, and Deindustrialization

Hard versus Soft Landings

Since the early 1980s, economists have failed rather dismally to construct convincing theoretical models of why the seemingly endless U.S. current-account deficits (figure 6.1) are sustained by a seemingly endless willingness of the rest of the world to acquire dollar assets. Reflecting this conceptual inadequacy, many see the continuation of such global "imbalances" to be unsustainable. Worriers claim that foreigners—both governments and their private sectors—will eventually cease buying dollar assets, which will trigger a collapse in the dollar's value in the foreign exchanges and in America's ability to borrow from foreigners. Beginning with the infamous twin deficits—fiscal and trade—of the Reagan presidency in the 1980s, such failed predictions have been commonplace for almost 30 years.

Alone among nations, the United States has a virtually unlimited line of credit with the rest of the world to sustain its current-account deficits because, in extremis, it could create the necessary international means of payment to repay debts to foreigners.

Figure 6.1.
The U.S. Current Account (% of GDP)
Source: Bureau of Economic Analysis

Consequently the U.S. can borrow heavily in its own currency because creditors of the United States voluntarily build up dollar claims—or are trapped into building up dollar claims, as we saw in chapter 5. Consequently, the net international wealth position of the United States (measured in dollars of course!) has become increasingly negative.

As of 2009, figure 6.2 shows that value of foreign claims on the United States (a large proportion of which are Treasury bonds) exceeds America's claims on foreigners (mainly equities and direct investments) by $2.5 to $3 trillion—mainly the cumulative effect of past current-account deficits. This large and growing net indebtedness of the United States continually confounds the prognosticators of the dollar's imminent collapse because they have seen less highly indebted countries in Asia and Latin America—and now Europe—ultimately being forced to repay in crisis circumstances associated with devaluations or default.

This resilience of the unloved dollar standard is even more astonishing in the aftermath of the Nixon, Carter, Greenspan, and Bernanke shocks to world monetary stability (chs. 4 and 5). True, the sharp decline in confidence in the euro since 2010

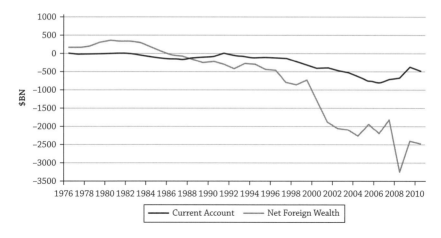

Figure 6.2.
U.S. Current Account and Net Foreign Wealth
Source: Bureau of Economic Analysis

undoubtedly buoyed the position of the dollar as international money—but this hardly explains the dollar's robustness for the previous 30 years. Apparently, having just one currency to facilitate international exchange has such great technical advantages in economizing on markets (ch. 2) that it overcomes the risks seen by the rest of the world of depending so heavily on that one national currency. And once it is ensconced as the central facilitator of international exchange, very powerful network effects take hold to keep the dollar as the prime vehicle currency in interbank markets. Although hardly satisfying, this nontechnical explanation of the persistence of the unloved dollar standard is the best I can do.

IS THE UNITED STATES ALSO TRAPPED?

That said, what have been the consequences for the United States itself of its unique ability to borrow from the rest of the world?

Foreign central banks now hold almost half the outstanding stock of U.S. Treasury bonds beyond the Fed's own holdings and that of other U.S. government agencies. The incidental effect has been to provide a cheap and very long line of dollar credit to the U.S. Treasury and U.S. economy more generally. Because the United States is the only country that can go deeply into debt in its *own* currency, it is invulnerable to the usual risk faced by other debtor countries whose debts are denominated in foreign currencies. Because the Federal Reserve Bank could potentially "print" enough dollars to repay the U.S. Treasury's foreign dollar debts, outright default is not a possibility.

Indeed, in international portfolios, U.S. Treasury bonds are generally treated as the world's "risk-free" financial assets against which risk premia in bonds denominated in other currencies are measured. And, with the big proviso that the U.S. price level remains fairly stable, foreign central banks are loath to see their currencies appreciate against the dollar. Today's very low nominal interest rates on dollar assets, from near 0 percent on short-term securities rising to just 2 percent on 10-year Treasury bonds (figures 5.1 and 5.2), suggest that the markets don't take U.S. default or depreciation risk very seriously—perhaps because so much of U.S. Treasury debt now resides in central banks—both domestic and foreign (ch. 5). Is this then nirvana for the saving-deficient, some might say profligate, United States?

Despite being at the center of the international dollar standard, the United States itself is also trapped by it—although not so obviously as its creditor countries on the dollar's periphery. This entrapment of the United States has longer- and shorter-run dimensions.

Consider the long-run problem first. To a considerable extent, low U.S. saving is a natural consequence of the ease with which it can borrow from foreigners. This ultrasoft borrowing constraint tilts the behavior of the federal government toward deficit spending because of the ease with which it can sell low-yield Treasury bonds to foreign financial institutions. But private borrowing can also be excessive.

In 2012, the American economy is now more fragile because of low U.S. domestic saving: meager personal saving has fallen to about 4 percent of GNP—less than half of what it was in the non-inflationary 1960s, and large government fiscal deficits are now nearly 9 percent of GNP—although the economy has partially recovered from its cyclical trough in 2008–09. Figure 6.3 shows the decline of America's long-term saving rate relative to China's rising rate. In the 1960s, U.S. gross saving was over 20 percent of GDP, whereas today it is less than 10 percent. America's current-account deficit of 4 to 5 percent of GDP simply reflects this long-term saving deficiency. America needs to borrow heavily in world markets in general, and from East Asia in particular, to prevent a domestic credit crunch that would sharply reduce U.S. investment—normally about 16 percent of U.S. GNP. So the United States is trapped in the sense that it needs the foreign finance to prevent a credit crunch.

U.S. domestic politics have taken a strange turn that reflects this soft borrowing constraint. The reckless political pressure

Figure 6.3.
U.S. and China Current Account and Gross Domestic Savings as Percentage of GDP
Source: World Bank, OECD, Stat

from so-called supply-siders to cut taxes, no matter what the budgetary consequences, could only be sustained for so long because the United States alone has virtually unlimited access to international credit denominated in its own currency to cover the resulting fiscal deficits. Other debtor economies face the specter of having debts build up in foreign currencies (largely dollars) that, if continued indefinitely, would provoke an attack on their currencies—as with the forced depreciations of the Indonesian, Korean, Malaysian, Philippine, and Thai currencies in 1997–98 or the Argentinian peso in 2002. Such an attack, or the threat thereof, then forces a retrenchment in the debtor country's government finances or private bank lending or both. But not so in the United States, where low national saving is endogenously determined because of its ultrasoft borrowing constraint.

In the shorter run, the real or imagined insufficiency of aggregate demand in the American economy induces the U.S. government to be ultra-Keynesian. Democrats or Republicans cut taxes or raise expenditures with alacrity at any sign of economic slack in the American economy. On February 14, 2012, President Obama submitted his 2012 budget to the U.S. Congress; it makes little or no progress in reducing America's saving deficiency, and it projects a fiscal deficit of over half a trillion dollars by 2015 and increasing thereafter.

In the world system, this soft borrowing constraint has induced the United States to be "the consumer of last resort." In 2012, Japan, Korea, and the euro area face a growth slowdown with deflation unless exports to the United States can be sustained—whence the willingness of emerging markets, especially China, to accumulate huge volumes of dollar exchange reserves to prevent their currencies from appreciating and slowing export growth (ch. 5). In 2011–12, the Bank of Japan intervened several times to buy dollars to dampen the unduly strong yen. This uncomfortable dependence of the United States on its foreign creditors is mutually symbiotic.

The U.S. government's "Keynesian"[1] proclivity to deficit-spend with every real or imagined cyclical downturn can only be accommodated because of America's unique position in the global monetary system. The international dollar standard relaxes the borrowing constraints on agents in the American economy, particularly households and the federal government, and lures them into feeling that they can safely get by without saving much.

THE DEINDUSTRIALIZATION OF THE UNITED STATES

But suppose that a crash in the unloved dollar standard, where a cessation of foreign lending to the United States precipitates a credit crunch, is avoided indefinitely. There remains an additional cost to the "trapped" center country: an untoward contraction in employment in its manufacturing sector. Heavy reliance on foreign borrowing speeds the pace of deindustrialization in the United States.

Employment in American manufacturing has been shrinking for a long time. In the mid-1960s, manufacturing output was 27 percent of GNP and its share of employment was 24 percent. By 2004, these numbers had fallen to about 13.8 percent and 10.1 percent, respectively—and in 2011, manufacturing employment had fallen to less than 9 percent of the U.S. labor force. Although not so dramatic as in the United States, the other advanced industrial countries also show marked shrinkage in the size of their manufacturing sectors. The consensus explanation is twofold: since the 1960s rapid technical progress has been greater in manufacturing than in services, and, as households become richer, demand naturally shifts away from goods toward services. Even with far fewer resources being allocated to manufacturing, modern economies are still in consumption equilibrium.

But how does foreign trade enter this consensus view? Stalwart free traders—such as Gregory Mankiw, then chairman of the

Council of Economic Advisors in the *Economic Report of the President* (February 2004)—argued that America's remarkable productivity growth, particularly in manufacturing, is the proximate reason for the shrinkage in the size of the manufacturing sector. Mankiw also argued that foreign competitive pressure, including outsourcing, increases technical progress in manufacturing. Weaker American manufacturing industries are being continually displaced, and manufacturing output becomes concentrated in more profitable and technically dynamic activities.

So, in the United States and other industrial economies, foreign trade shrinks the size of manufacturing sectors indirectly by benignly increasing the pace of technical progress—rather than (malignly) by direct displacement of workers without increasing the economy's overall ability to reabsorb them. According to Mankiw, the outsourcing of jobs in manufacturing and services—however ominous it might seem—is simply the modern manifestation of healthy ongoing international competition.

This standard defense of free trade is well and good as far as it goes. However, it fails to link the unusual shrinkage in manufacturing employment to America's saving deficiency. Heavy foreign borrowing aggravates the natural decline in the size of the U.S. manufacturing sector well beyond that experienced by other mature industrial countries, which generally are not net borrowers internationally.

The transfer of foreign saving to the United States is embodied more in goods than in services. India aside, most services are not so easily traded internationally. Thus when American spending rises above output (income), the net absorption of foreign goods—largely raw materials and manufactures—increases. True, episodic sharp increases in the price of oil significantly increase the U.S. current-account deficit for awhile. However, figure 6.4 shows that, since the early 1980s, the trade deficit in manufactures alone has been about as big as the current-account deficit, that is, as big as America's saving shortfall.

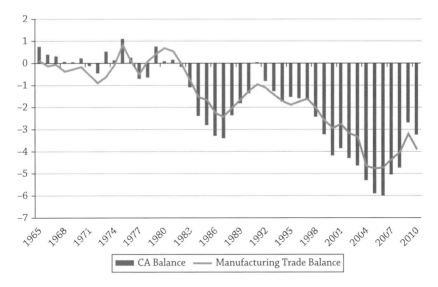

Figure 6.4.
U.S. Current-Account Balance and Trade Balance in Manufacturing, 1965–2010
(% of GDP)
Source: Bureau of Economic Analysis

Highly industrialized economies in East Asia, such as Japan and China, have had big saving (trade) surpluses—and are the natural creditors of the saving-deficient United States. Because their exports are largely manufactures, the real counterpart of their buildup of nominal dollar claims is for them to run export surpluses in manufactures with the United States—as shown in figure 6.4. This "transfer problem" is discussed in more depth in chapter 9.

THE SHRINKAGE IN AMERICAN MANUFACTURING

We can estimate very roughly the shrinkage in American manufacturing from its saving deficiency by making simplifying assumptions. Assume that spending by American households and firms for manufactures is more or less independent of whether the goods are produced at home or abroad. Then domestic production of manufactures shrinks by the amount of the trade deficit in manufactures. The consequent loss in jobs depends inversely on labor productivity in manufacturing, which rises strongly through time. The actual path of manufacturing employment from 1965 to 2009 is the unbroken dark line in figure 6.5.

If we take the trade deficit in manufactures and add it back to get "adjusted manufactured output," and assume that labor productivity (output per person) is the same in adjusted output as in actual output, we get projected employment in manufacturing—the dashed line in figure 6.5. For example, in 2004, actual employment in manufacturing was just 10.1 percent of the American labor force, but it would have been 14 percent without a trade deficit in manufactures. The difference is 4 to 5 million lost jobs in manufacturing. In 2009, actual employment in manufacturing was about 8.5 percent of the labor force and the simulated employment assuming no saving deficiency, that is, balanced trade, was about 10.3 percent.

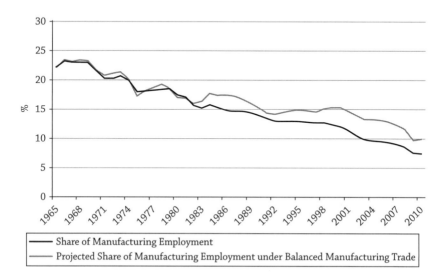

Figure 6.5.
Projection of Labor Growth in U.S. Manufacturing under Balanced Manufacturing Trade, 1965–2010
Source: Bureau of Economic Analysis, author's projection

As early as the 1980s, employment in manufacturing began to shrink substantially because of the then large current-account deficit (figure 6.1) attributed to the then large fiscal deficit: the famous twin deficits of Ronald Reagan's presidency. With fiscal consolidation in the 1990s under President Clinton, the saving gap narrowed but wasn't closed because American personal saving weakened. Now under Presidents George W. Bush and Barack Obama, the fiscal deficit has exploded while private saving still remains weak. The result is heavy borrowing from foreigners, leading to all-time highs in the U.S. current-account deficit in 2005 (figure 6.1). The main component remains the trade deficit in manufactures, leading to intensified shrinkage in American manufacturing employment.

Should we be concerned? Note that I am not suggesting that the trend in overall U.S. unemployment has increased (although it may have), but only that its composition has been tilted away from manufactures. In the past, the U.S. economy remained a very efficient job-creating machine, with growth in service-sector employment largely offsetting the decline in manufacturing. However, the rate of technical change in manufacturing is much higher than in other sectors. And it is hard to imagine the U.S. sustaining its technical leadership with no manufacturing sector at all.

More uncomfortably, more congressmen, pundits, and voters feel justified in claiming that foreigners use unfair trade practices to steal American jobs, particularly in manufacturing. In lobbying against free trade, protectionists use the supposed undervaluing of their exchange rates by East Asian countries (particularly China), the poor working conditions in countries that are naturally poor, and so on, as pretexts for imposing tariffs or other restraints on manufactured imports into the United States. But this critique of foreigners is misplaced when net American imports of manufactures is primarily a consequence of America's saving deficiency. Better to lobby the U.S. government to reduce its fiscal deficit.

THE LONG WAY OUT: THE SOFT-LANDING SCENARIO

There is no easy way out of the worldwide dollar standard trap. A deep devaluation of the dollar from its historical norms will only worsen macroeconomic conditions, deflation on the periphery or inflation in the United States, within the trap *without* springing it. Chapters 7 and 8 show the futility of trying to "correct" a trade imbalance, which only reflects international saving imbalances, by changing the exchange rate. So what can be done?

The most promising, although still difficult, way out is to change the saving behavior of the United States over the next decade or two. Immediate large increases in taxes or cuts in government expenditure are not desirable from today's countercyclical point of view. Instead a slow and deliberate improvement in the U.S. public finances from deficit to surplus with a strong improvement in the propensity to save of American households—perhaps through tax incentives and higher required down payments for automobile and home purchases—is devoutly to be wished.

However, a necessary complement to gradually increasing American net saving is to have "surplus" saving abroad gradually decline. And here the behavior of China is all important. Chapters 12 and 13 show that, in recent years, the share of enterprise profits in Chinese GDP has grown sharply relative to the disposable income of Chinese households. Thus a parallel gradual shift from enterprise profits (which are largely saved) to household disposable income would reduce surplus saving in China, and make the soft landing even softer.

A HARD-LANDING SCENARIO WITH A CREDIT CRUNCH: A NATURAL EXPERIMENT IN 1991–92

Ironically, if American protectionists succeed and imports from foreigners were suddenly greatly reduced so as to prevent the transfer of foreign saving to the United States, the U.S. fiscal deficit would be uncovered and a credit crunch would ensue—with greater losses of American jobs. To illustrate this important point, a sharp fall in the inflow of foreign finance to the saving-deficient United States did occur in 1991–92—and did lead to a cessation of bank lending to firms and households. The resulting sharp economic downturn prevented George H. Bush, who was otherwise a very successful president, from being reelected in the fall of 1992.

This natural experiment of what happens when long-term capital inflows suddenly cease, and imports fall sharply relative to exports, shows up in figure 6.1: the U.S. current-account deficit temporarily vanished in late 1991 before deepening again to its "norm" after 1992. At that time, Japan and Germany were by far America's largest creditors with current-account surpluses—and both were buffeted coincidentally by exogenous negative shocks to their lending capabilities, which had nothing to do with each other or with economic events in the United States. This little recognized explanation of the otherwise mysterious U.S. credit crunch of 1991–92 was written up with supporting figures and analysis in a book I wrote with Kenichi Ohno (McKinnon and Ohno 1997)—and I can do no better than reproduce some of its essentials.

Germany in 1991 after the Fall of the Berlin Wall in 1990

"The fiscal costs of reunification changed Germany almost overnight from being a big international lender up to 1990 to being a net borrower in 1991....Germany's current-account surplus fell from about $50 billion per year before 1991 to a *deficit* of about $20 billion in 1991" (McKinnon and Ohno 1997, 120).

Japan in 1991 and the Collapse in Its Bubble Economy

"The crash in the Japanese stock and property markets so impaired the capital positions of important Japanese financial institutions—banks, insurance companies, trust funds, and so on—that they shifted out of long-term international lending.... [L]ong-term capital was actually repatriated to Japan in 1991 before a very modest recovery began 1992.... Not only was the amount of foreign capital available to the American economy suddenly reduced because of the Japanese financial crash, but the form of finance shifted dramatically from long term to short term" (McKinnon and Ohno 1997, 120).

McKinnon and Ohno go much further in analyzing the interest rate effects within the American financial system from this double shock of German reunification and the bursting of the Japanese stock and property market bubbles. In effect, the sudden drying up of foreign purchases of long-term U.S. Treasuries in the face of a large ongoing U.S. fiscal deficit meant that long-term interest rates rose sharply and induced American banks to buy Treasury bonds instead of lending normally to businesses for working capital, whence the intense "credit crunch" and sharp U.S. economic downturn in 1991–92.

Of course, after 1992, foreign capital from many sources began to return to the United States—and the U.S. fiscal deficit moderated for some years. For the remainder of the 1990s, the American capital market was restored as banks returned to normal lending to firms and households and the economy recovered and the trade deficit widened.

Nevertheless, the credit crunch of 1991–92 usefully illustrates what could happen if foreign creditors—now mainly emerging markets (EMs) such a Brazil and China—were induced *collectively* to stop lending to the United States. Instead of intervening in the foreign exchange markets to buy dollars (as described in chapter 5), suppose EM central banks just stepped back and let their currencies appreciate in the face of the Fed's zero-interest-rate policy. If somehow they did it by common agreement, no one EM would be particularly disadvantaged from having its currency appreciate against the others. However, because they would no longer be significant buyers of U.S. Treasuries, the now much larger U.S. fiscal deficit would again be uncovered.

So I leave it to the reader to imagine how a new credit crunch from this hypothetical withdrawal of foreign financial support from the United States would work itself out. Of course, the probability of such collective action among diverse nations is small. However, now in 2012, China bulks very large. As I speculate in chapter 13, China with its stable dollar exchange rate is key in holding the world's dollar-based monetary system together. If the People's Bank of China wearies of seemingly unending purchases of low-yield dollar assets in order to stabilize its exchange rate, other emerging markets would surely follow.

NOTES

1. With apologies to the memory of Keynes himself, who, if alive today, might not be a Keynesian.

CHAPTER 7

༄

Exchange Rates and Trade Balances under the Dollar Standard

HONG (HELEN) QIAO

In this chapter, we consider the impacts of discrete exchange rate changes in open economies with net foreign exchange liabilities and assets under the dollar standard. To anticipate the results of the investigation, the combination of wealth, price, investment, and indirect investment effects (when present) increases the complexity of predicting current-account movements following exchange rate changes, which in many cases leads to ambiguous results. For instance, currency devaluation may well improve the trade balance of a debtor economy by depressing domestic absorption, whereas an appreciation has an ambiguous effect on the trade balance of a creditor economy. Because exchange rate changes can no longer be separated from domestic price-level and absorption effects, except in special cases, they cannot be used predictably to adjust the trade balance.

Let us now put a foundation under these conclusions.

Some commentators in the Western financial press have suggested that East Asian economies, especially China, have undervalued currencies and should seek to appreciate them (Lardy 2003, 2005; Goldstein 2004; Roubini 2005). To reduce trade surpluses, especially in bilateral trade with the United States, these economies are advised to appreciate or freely float their currencies in the near future (Lardy 2005). Instead of addressing the external imbalances by increasing national savings (public and private), the U.S. government willingly and conveniently adopted this simplistic view, and has exerted pressures on China and other East Asian trading partners to adjust their exchange rate policies. This chapter shows that the U.S. trade deficit would not necessarily be alleviated by forcing creditor countries to appreciate.

Most economists who propose to use exchange rate changes to adjust trade balances have elasticities models in mind, which are based on insular economies from the past rather than the open economies of today. However, unlike the industrial economies after World War II, now countries are much more open, with a greater trade component and impressive inflows and outflows of capital. Notably, open economies react differently to exchange rate changes than insular ones do. McKinnon (1990) and McKinnon and Ohno (1997) have shown that in open economies, exchange rate changes may have unpredictable effects on trade balances. In other words, with the correct setup of open-economy models, depreciation may not improve the trade balance, and appreciation may not worsen it.

This chapter traces out the effects of exogenous exchange changes on open creditor/debtor economies when income and absorption are endogenously determined. It reveals that the combination of wealth effect and investment effect, together with the indirect investment effect (in the East Asian region), increases the complexity of forecasting current-account movements accompanying any exchange rate change. Except for the case when a debtor economy depreciates its currency against the dollar and suffers a foreign exchange crisis that depresses the economy, it is impossible to predict the net trade balance effect of a depreciation or appreciation because absorption may move "perversely" and offset the relative price effects.

Chapter 9 in this book tackles the problem the other way around. To correct a trade imbalance, suppose government(s) act exogenously and in concert to change domestic absorption. The deficit country raises taxes and cuts spending, while the surplus country cuts taxes or otherwise increases spending. However, the exchange rate is left to be determined endogenously. As chapter 9 shows, the resulting improvement in the trade balance need not—and it is better if it does not—induce the deficit country's currency to depreciate, contrary to the expectations of conventional theory.

LITERATURE REVIEW

As with many other subjects in economics, economists have yet to reach an agreement over whether equilibrium in the balance of payments can be reached by exchange rate changes. But unlike other projects that require economists and politicians to work together, in this case the misconception of adjusting trade balances through exchange rate movements can be largely attributed to economists, not politicians. Most economists who believe that exchange rate changes systematically affect trade balances acquired such thinking from the conventional elasticities model of the balance of trade, which is still being taught in undergraduate economic courses today.

Created in the 1930s and still widely accepted, the elasticities approach is central to many Keynesian (Meade 1951) and monetarist models (Friedman 1953; Johnson 1958). According to these models, the exchange rate is assigned to address external balance, while government expenditures are assigned to internal balance and full employment. However, this type of model is based on the assumption that exchange rate policies can be separated from monetary policies and investment decisions. In other words, it is assumed that when a discrete exchange rate change takes place, the domestic price level can remain undisturbed because the money supply is unaffected. In some circumstances, this may be true. For example, among the industrial countries after World War II, when capital movement was strictly limited and trade was less prevalent, this separability in policy was possible. In that case, a currency depreciation may lead to a reduction in a trade deficit, and an appreciation lead to a reduction in a trade surplus.

However, no one will deny that today industrial economies and emerging market economies are much more open than they were 50 years ago. Without the insularity assumption, the elasticity type of model is no longer valid in predicting the consequences of exchange rate changes (McKinnon 1990, 1997). Nonetheless, economic scholars have yet to update their framework of assumptions when they naturally associate currency depreciations with current-account deficit reduction. For example, in a recent publication of the Institute for International Economics, Goldstein (2004) concluded that "To reduce the U.S. current-account deficit to, say, 2 to 2½ percent of GDP at reasonable cost, it would be helpful to have a real depreciation of the dollar of about 25 percent from its peak (in February 2002)," which is based on "the rule of thumb that each 1 percent fall in the real trade-weighted dollar improves the U.S. current-account position by roughly $10 billion." Clearly, he remains a strong supporter of the elasticities model: "As James Meade (1951) emphasized more than 50 years ago, the classical remedy for an economy experiencing both domestic overheating and external surpluses is exchange rate appreciation, and neither reserve nor debt consideration appear to constrain such exchange rate action."

It perhaps will take years—and, one hopes, not too many more mistakes—for the elasticity school to realize that a discrete change in exchange rate does not necessarily lead to trade balance adjustment in a certain direction. In open economies today, capital markets are no longer tightly restricted, and interest rates are influenced by expected exchange rate changes. As a result, exchange rate determination can no longer be isolated from monetary policies nor from the level of domestic investment.

According to Frenkel and Mussa (1980), in an open economy, the exchange rate is a forward-looking variable. They adopt an asset-market approach that implies that investors will base their port-folio decisions between claims denominated in local and foreign currencies on their expectations of future exchange rates. Thus, their portfolio decisions determine today's spot exchange rates.

How do people form their expectations on future exchange rates in the first place? They are ultimately derived from expecta-tions on the relative tightness of monetary policies in one country compared to others. If they feel that future monetary policy will be tighter in a certain country than elsewhere, the price level in this country will decrease, while the demand for its currency grows, which forces an appreciation in the spot market, and investment falls. In other words, in an open economy, exchange rates are endogenous to present and future monetary polices and so is the domestic investment decision. Unless the monetary authority accommodates the private sector's expectation on future monetary policy, exchange rate changes will not be sus-tainable. Therefore, it seems rather simplistic to ignore the monetary and domestic investment consequences from an exchange rate change (as is done in an elasticities model).

McKinnon (1990) and McKinnon and Ohno (1997) have dem-onstrated that exchange rate changes may be followed by unpre-dictable movements of the balance of payments in open economies. Under the dollar standard in the twenty-first century, how should exchange rate economics be updated for open econ-omies with large dollar assets or debts? What are the distinctive features of economies in East Asia and how are they related to the East Asian financial crisis? In discussing the impact of dis-crete exchange rate changes, this chapter addresses these ques-tions by introducing a wealth effect, an investment effect, and an indirect investment effect into relevant macroeconomic models.

INSULAR VERSUS OPEN ECONOMIES

Let's first review the differences between insular and open economies by analyzing the short-term and long-term effect of an exchange rate change within each.

Insular Economies

Defined in the same fashion as in McKinnon (1990) and McKinnon and Ohno (1997), an insular economy in the following model reflects industrial countries from the 1930s to 1950s, and some developing countries at a later time. Such an economy features a tightly regulated capital market and domestically determined interest rates. The trade component in the economy is also limited so that exchange rate changes affect trade volume but not the domestic price level.

The setup of the insular-economy model is borrowed from McKinnon (1997) with reference to Marston (1985). Lowercase letters are logarithms

$$Y = A + B \qquad \text{Domestic output} \qquad (1)$$

$$A = C(Y) + I(\underset{-}{i - \dot{p}}) + G \qquad \text{Domestic absorption} \qquad (2)$$

$$B = B(\underset{-}{A}, \underset{+}{e - p}) \qquad \text{Trade balance} \qquad (3)$$

$$m - p = L(\underset{+\ -\ -}{Y, i, \dot{p}}) \qquad \text{Money market} \qquad (4)$$

$$\dot{p} = \alpha\left(Y - \overline{Y}\right), (\alpha > 0) \qquad \text{Price equation} \qquad (5)$$

$$p = \overline{p} \qquad \text{Alternative price equation} \qquad (6)$$

where endogenous variables include $Y, A, B, p\,(\dot{p}\,)$, and i and exogenous variables include $G, e, \overline{Y}$, and m. In this standard macroeconomic model and its modifications in the following section, variables are defined as shown in box 7.1.

Assume that the nominal exchange rate is exogenously determined in an arrangement resembling dollar pegs. The real exchange rate is equal to $e - p$, as the foreign price p^* is assumed to be fixed.

There are two alternative equations for domestic price determination: (5) and (6). Equation (5) allows the price to respond to a deviation of the full-employment output level. And equation (6) fixes the price at the level of $\overline{p}$. In this insular economy, exchange rate changes cannot be passed on to domestic prices through either of the two price equations. In addition, the exchange rate does not affect domestic absorption directly because domestic investment is not influenced by the real exchange rate and the domestic interest rate is isolated from foreign ones. There are neither foreign-currency assets nor debts, that is, $F = 0$. In the following part, we will adopt equation (5) for price determination in our model. However, if this price equation is replaced by equation (6), it should not affect our results in any significant way.

Box 7.1

NOTATION FOR MODEL OF THE INSULAR ECONOMY

Y	= real GDP	$\overline{Y}$	= full-employment output
A	= domestic absorption	B	= trade balance (net)
i	= domestic interest rate	i^*	= foreign interest rate
p	= domestic price level	$\dot{p}$	= price level change
G	= government expenditure	e	= nominal exchange rate (domestic currency/ foreign currency)
m	= domestic money supply	F	= foreign currency assets

To determine the sign of the derivative of the trade balance with respect to changes in the real exchange rate, we have to consider both the direct impact and the indirect effect from domestic absorption. Let us first examine the direct impact from an exchange rate change. Suppose the partial derivative of the trade balance with respect to the real exchange rate is positive: that the well-known Marshall-Lerner condition is satisfied, that is,

$$\frac{\partial B}{\partial(e-p)} > 0.$$

That means, ceteris paribus, the exchange rate will affect the trade balance in the same way as predicted by conventional wisdom. A real depreciation of the local currency makes imports more expensive and exports cheaper, thus boosting exports and reducing imports, improving the current-account balance. Vice versa, an appreciation encourages imports and reduces exports, thus lowering the current-account surplus.

In this model of an insular economy, we now have to consider the domestic absorption effect from the impact of currency depreciation on domestic expenditure. In the insular economy, the domestic money supply can be fixed, while the unliberalized capital account permits exchange rate changes. In this economy, a devaluation stimulates exports and income, while domestic absorption is constrained by the fixed money supply. As output increases, the interest rate rises ($\frac{di}{de} > 0$), which restrains domestic absorption. In the end, the increase in output is more pronounced than the increase in absorption, and thus trade balance still improves after considering domestic absorption effects.

$$\frac{dY}{de} > \frac{dA}{de} \rightarrow \frac{dB}{de} > 0$$

In the long run, however, the price change induced by depreciation diminishes as prices remain at the higher level, $\dot{p} \rightarrow 0$ and $p \uparrow$.

Table 7.1. INSULAR ECONOMY: DEPRECIATION/APPRECIATION AGAINST
DOLLAR (NO NET FOREIGN EXCHANGE INDEBTEDNESS)

	Wealth Effect	Investment Effect	Domestic Absorption	Import	Export	Trade Balance
Depreciation	-	-	↑ (small and limited)	↓	↑	↑
Appreciation	-	-	↓ (small and limited)	↑	↓	↓

Such a price increase reduces the real money supply, inducing an increase in the interest rate because of the money market equilibrium. This is easily seen from equation (4). As output falls back to the original level in the long run, the domestic interest rate is the only adjustable variable to accommodate the fall in the real money supply from the higher price levels. In other words, the interest rate has to rise, which reduces domestic investment (and domestic absorption) according to equation (2), improving the trade balance also in the long run.

Table 7.1 summarizes the impact effects of an exchange rate change in an insular economy systematically.

Open Economies

As readers must have noticed, the insular features of the economy described in the previous section bear very few similarities to the ones prevailing today. Now there is a much higher proportion of international trade, and current rules against capital movements internationally are much less restrictive than 50 years ago. Now exchange rates can float more freely if governments choose to let them. Almost all industrial countries after the 1960s and many emerging market economies today are better described by the following model for open economies.

$$i = i^*$$ Interest rate parity   (7)

$$\dot{p} = \beta(e - p), \text{where}(\beta > 0)$$ Price expectation   (8)

$$Y = A + B$$ Domestic output   (9)

$$A = C(Y) + I(i - \dot{p}, e - p) + G$$ Domestic absorption   (10)
$$\qquad\quad + - +$$

$$B = B(A, e - p)$$ Trade balance   (11)
$$\qquad - +$$

$$m - p = L(Y, i, \dot{p})$$ Money market   (12)
$$\qquad\quad + - -$$

Endogenous variables are Y, A, B, p ($\dot{p}$), m, and i; exogenous variables are e, i^*, and G.

An open economy differs from an insular one, and this is reflected in the setup of the model. In the first place, equation (7) states that the domestic interest rate has to follow the international one. In this model of stationary exchange rate expectations, risk adjustments are omitted. Financial openness requires the rate of return or domestic bond yield to converge to the international level.

Second, price equation (8) pinpoints that the real exchange rate should lead domestic prices. According to the asset-market approach of exchange rate determination (Frenkel and Mussa 1980, 1985), today's exchange rate changes can affect future domestic price levels through the expectation of future changes in monetary policies. The reason is that any substantial exchange rate change can only be sustained by future monetary adjustments permitting price level changes at home (or the opposite changes abroad).

On the output side, both domestic absorption and the trade balance are influenced by real exchange rate changes. In particular, currency depreciation raises inflation expectations and lowers the real interest rate, which gives a boost to domestic investment. In addition, the drop in currency value also makes the economy a less expensive place in which to invest. At the same time, if a currency appreciates, investment in that country will likely slow as a result of higher real interest rates and the relatively higher price of on-site investments compared to those in other economies. The relationship between real exchange rate changes and investment/domestic absorption can be summarized as the follows:

$$\frac{\partial I}{\partial (e-p)} > 0.$$

Suppose there is an unexpected appreciation, which is discrete and isolated from other major policy changes in government expenditure, and money supply changes exogenously. In the short run, $\dot{p}$ becomes negative according to equation (8), but p initially remains at its original level. The appreciation in the exchange rate does not affect the domestic interest rate, which is aligned with the foreign rates. Therefore we have

$$e - p \downarrow i - p \uparrow \text{and } \dot{p} < 0.$$

Such real appreciation together with an increase in the real interest rate slows down domestic investment, as described in equation (10). Domestic absorption A and imports both decrease along with exports, leaving the sign of trade balance $B = Y - A$ indeterminate. In the short term, before the domestic price level falls, the responses to an exogenous exchange rate appreciation in an open economy with anticipated future accommodation of domestic monetary policy can be summarized as follows:

$$\frac{d\dot{p}}{de} < 0, \frac{dY}{de} < 0, \frac{dA}{de} < 0, \frac{dB}{de} 0.$$

Table 7.2. OPEN ECONOMIES: INITIAL IMPACT OF A DISCRETE EXCHANGE RATE CHANGE

	Wealth Effect	Investment Effect	Domestic Absorption	Import	Export	Trade Balance
Depreciation	-	↑	↑	↑	↑	?
Appreciation	-	↓	↓	↓	↓	?

If it still seems less than obvious why currency appreciation does not necessarily lead to a reduction in trade surplus, let us try to explain it without the help of equations. Suppose the Marshall-Lerner condition is still satisfied, that is, the price effect from real appreciation will cause an increase in imports and a slump in exports, reducing the overall trade surplus. On the other hand, this appreciation also makes the economy a more expensive place in which to invest, and at the same time exerts a tightening effect on the domestic economy due to the deflationary pressure. As a result, growth of investment and output moderates, triggering a deceleration in domestic demand and imports. Although exports slow down as a result of the currency appreciation, imports also decline, making the net impact on trade balance ambiguous. Conversely, currency depreciation in an open economy does not necessarily improve the trade balance either.

We list the short-term effects of discrete exchange rate changes in an open economy above in table 7.2. In contrast to the effects on an insular economy in table 7.1, the net effect on trade balance is ambiguous.

Since we assume the central bank accommodates the private sector's expectation on future monetary policy, which is embedded in the exchange rate, the future path for the money supply should be endogenously determined by the exchange rate change and the rate of price change. In the special but simplest case of a discrete appreciation with no change in the interest rate and no discrete change in today's money supply, the vector of changes in future money supplies can be described as follows:

$$m_t = p_t + L(Y_t, i_t, \dot{p}_t)$$

$$m_{t+1} = p_{t+1} + L(Y_{t+1}, i_{t+1}, \dot{p}_{t+1}) = p_t(1 + \dot{p}_t) + L(Y_{t+1}, i_{t+1}, \dot{p}_{t+1})$$

$$m_{t+2} = p_{t+2} + L(Y_{t+2}, i_{t+2}, \dot{p}_{t+2}) = p_t(1 + \dot{p}_t)(1 + \dot{p}_{t+1}) + L(Y_{t+2}, i_{t+2}, \dot{p}_{t+2})$$

$$\dots$$

$$m_{t+n} = p_{t+n} + L(Y_{t+n}, i_{t+n}, \dot{p}_{t+n}) = p_t \prod_{i=0}^{n}(1 + \dot{p}_{t+i}) + L(Y_{t+n}, i_{t+n}, \dot{p}_{t+n})$$

As the economy approaches a new steady state, the money supply would have to decrease in strict proportion to e (and to p). Otherwise, e will have to depreciate back to its original level as the monetary policy becomes inconsistent with people's expectations. The effect on expected future money supplies is illustrated in figure 7.1.

In the long run, however, any discrete change in the nominal exchange rate eventually washes out as the domestic price level increases so as to restore the initial value of the real exchange

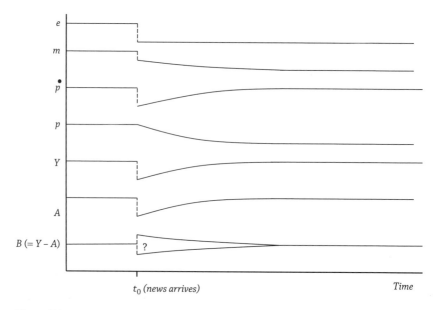

t_0 *(news arrives)*   *Time*

Figure 7.1.
An Open Economy's Response to an Exogenous Exchange Rate Appreciation with Anticipation of Monetary Tightening in the Future

rate. After PPP is restored, output, domestic absorption, and trade balance will be left unchanged, while prices and money supply remain at a lower level.

$$\frac{dY}{de} = \frac{dA}{de} = \frac{dB}{de} = 0, \frac{dp}{de} = \frac{dm}{de} = 1.$$

DEBTORS VERSUS CREDITORS UNDER THE DOLLAR STANDARD

The model in the previous section is a better depiction of the major economies in the 1970s and 1980s into the new millennium than is our first model. During those times, the global capital market was more or less symmetrical because neither the United States nor Japan (and certainly not China) had accumulated large dollar debts or assets. Nonetheless, the world has changed tremendously under the dollar standard over the past many years. As mentioned earlier, many economies have acquired significantly different positions in foreign-currency-denominated wealth. In the case of East Asia, a few countries have run chronic current-account surpluses, whereas others changed from net dollar debtors to creditors only recently. How does this difference in net wealth denominated in a foreign currency alter the impact of an exchange rate change on the trade balance?

To incorporate the asymmetry created by the dollar standard into the model, we expand the model into a two-country setup to include the economy with net foreign exchange assets—as denoted by F—and the United States. When $F < 0$, the economy is a net debtor. The rest of the world is treated as a sink so that the sum of world trade balances is zero.

$i = i^* + \gamma$ Interest rate parity   (13)

$\dot{p} = \beta(e - p), (\beta > 0)$ Price expectation   (14)

$$Y = A + B \qquad\qquad\qquad \text{Domestic output} \qquad (15)$$

$$A = C(Y, e \cdot F) + I(i - \dot{p}, e - p) + G \quad \text{Domestic absorption} \qquad (16)$$
$${+ + +} \;\; {-} \;\; {+}$$

$$B = B(A, e - p, A^{*}) \qquad\qquad \text{Trade balance} \qquad (17)$$
$${- + +}$$

$$m - p = L(Y, i, \dot{p}) \qquad\qquad \text{Money market} \qquad (18)$$
$${+ - -}$$

Endogenous variables are Y, A, B, p ($\dot{p}$), m, and i; exogenous variables are e, i^{*}, G, γ, and F

It is notable that the major differences between this economy of interest and the open economy introduced in the previous section are, first, that a wealth effect is included in domestic absorption (equation 16), and, second, U.S. absorption A^{*} will also affect the domestic economy's trade surplus (equation 17). The wealth effect has a positive impact on consumption, which implies that an appreciation decreases net wealth in domestic-currency terms for a creditor economy where $F > 0$. But for a debtor economy where $F < 0$, a depreciation increases net debt in domestic-currency terms. In both cases, people are conscious of such a change in their net wealth and reduce their consumption accordingly. Thus, for a creditor economy where $F > 0$, this negative wealth effect from an appreciation reinforces the investment effect (the investment slump) so that imports decline further. The net trade surplus of an appreciating creditor economy could actually increase!

The U.S. Economy

$$Y^{*} = A^{*} + B^{*} \qquad \text{Domestic output} \qquad\qquad (19)$$

$$A^{*} = C(Y^{*}) + I(i^{*} - \dot{p}^{*}, e^{*} - p^{*}) + G^{*} \qquad \text{Domestic absorption} \quad (20)$$
$$\phantom{A^{*} = C(Y^{*}) + I(}{-} \;\; {+}$$

$$B^* = B(A^*, e^* - p^*, A) \qquad \text{Trade balance} \qquad (21)$$
$$\quad\; - + +$$

$$m^* - p^* = L(Y^*, i^*, \dot{p}^*) \qquad \text{Money market} \qquad (22)$$
$$\quad\; + - -$$

$$\dot{p} = \alpha\left(Y^* - \overline{Y}^*\right), (\alpha > 0) \qquad \text{Price equation} \qquad (23)$$

Endogenous variables are Y^*, A^*, B^*, p^* ($\dot{p}^*$), and i^*; exogenous variables are G^*, e^*, $\overline{Y}^*$, m^*, and γ.

The asymmetry of the dollar standard is largely reflected in the fact that the U.S. economy bears more similarity to an insular economy than to an open economy. First, the U.S. interest rate i^* is determined domestically, and there is no direct impact on domestic price level from an exchange rate change (equation 23). Second, domestic absorption is not influenced by the net foreign indebtedness of the United States (equation 20) because all liquid foreign assets and debts are denominated in dollars.[1] We believe this setting describes the United States more accurately because of its central role in the world monetary system today.

Unlike interest rates in peripheral countries, the interest rate on dollar assets is determined in the U.S. market. The price level in the center country is also less affected by exchange rate changes because the dollar has served as the major invoice currency in international trade. Therefore the price equation adopted (equation 23) is different from that of the peripheral economy (equation 14) or the zero-debt open economy (equation 11).

The United States has a colossal amount of foreign debt, but primarily denominated in dollars. We acknowledge that some of the U.S. foreign claims are in other currencies, such as the euro, but the size of the claims is much smaller than dollar debts. Exchange rate changes may influence investment decisions in the United States because of the price effect, but due to the absence of the wealth effect, not the consumption decision.

The Rest of the World

$$B_r + B + B^* = 0. \qquad \text{World trade balance} \qquad (24)$$

DEBTOR COUNTRY'S DEPRECIATION AGAINST THE DOLLAR

Consider an economy with net foreign debts, largely denominated in dollars. Such debts have been accumulated from past current-account deficits. Suppose an unexpected event (such as a new administration committed to more extensive monetary expansion) takes place, leading to currency depreciation. Such depreciation will be sustained in the future if the monetary authority increases the money supply as per initial expectations.

In the short run, noticeably, a discrete depreciation sets off inflationary expectations and price increases in the debtor economy (equation 14). In response, domestic investment rises because of the drop in real interest rates and currency undervaluation (equation 16). Even though this leads to a rise in output, the economy's net worth decreases sharply because the domestic cost of dollar debts increases as a result of currency depreciation. Ultimately domestic consumption declines (equation 16), causing a slump in domestic absorption: the net trade balance of a debtor economy improves with devaluation.

The trade balance improvement can also be seen from the fact that after currency depreciation, exports grow and imports decline due to the price effect. The negative wealth effect then dominates the positive investment effect, setting a brake on domestic absorption. Domestic demand for imports slows down because

Table 7.3. DEBTOR'S DEPRECIATION AGAINST DOLLAR

	Wealth Effect	Investment Effect	Domestic Absorption	Import	Export	Trade Balance
Debtor	↓↓	↑	↓	↓	↑	↑
U.S.	-	↓	↓	↓	↓	?
Rest of world						↓

people restrain their consumption after finding out their net worth (in foreign exchange) decreases (through an increase in debt or a decrease in the value of assets). Therefore, both the price effect and the wealth effect dominate the investment effect and imports decrease, improving the trade balance. These short- to middle-term dynamics can be summarized as shown in table 7.3.

In the long run when the real exchange rate and PPP are restored, however, currency depreciation will leave output, domestic absorption, and the trade balance unchanged, while prices remain at a higher level (as price changes diminish). The money supply also increases as a result of the accommodating monetary policies.

$$\frac{dY}{de} = 0, \frac{dA}{de} = 0, \frac{dB}{de} = 0, \text{ and} \frac{dp}{de} = \frac{dm}{de} = 1.$$

Empirical results also support these theoretical predictions. Milesi-Ferretti and Razin (1998) recorded episodes of trade balance improvement following depreciations in Latin America and East Asia in the 1980s and 1990s. Notably, Colombia in 1982, Korea in 1984–86, Malaysia in 1986, and Thailand in 1984–86 were featured with policy shifts that drove down exchange rates. Without exception, these debtor economies improved their trade balances with stronger saving and a fall in absorption.

Reduction in trade deficits is more evident for debtor economies during crisis periods. Chile in 1983 and Mexico in 1982 and 1995 were known for sharp output contractions and substantial exchange rate depreciations. At the same time, investment fell because of the failing financial sector. Furthermore, domestic absorption declined in these debtor economies, making room for trade balance improvements following currency depreciations.

These economies are not alone. During the 1997–98 East Asian financial crisis, the five crisis economies (Korea, Malaysia, Indonesia, Thailand, and Philippines) all experienced remarkable improvement in their trade balances after their sharp depreciations reduced domestic absorption, as the cost of servicing their foreign debts greatly increased. Figures 7.2–7.7 illustrate their trade balances and exchange rate changes of between 1978 and 2005. Very much as Noland et al. (1998) argued, "net exports increase primarily through a compression of imports and only secondarily through an expansion of exports." These five crisis countries therefore had substantial improvements in their trade balances.

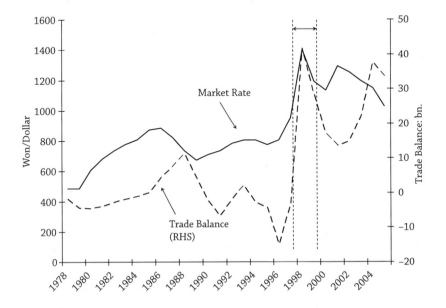

Figure 7.2.
Korea: Trade Balance and Exchange Rate

Figure 7.3.
Malaysia: Trade Balance and Exchange Rate

Figure 7.4.
Indonesia: Trade Balance and Exchange Rate

Figure 7.5.
Thailand: Trade Balance and Exchange Rate

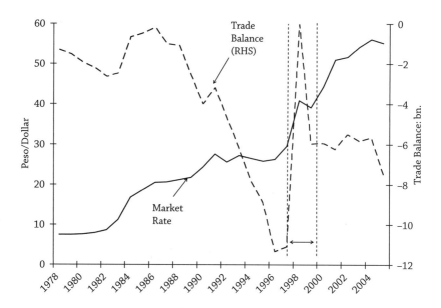

Figure 7.6.
Philippines: Trade Balance and Exchange Rate

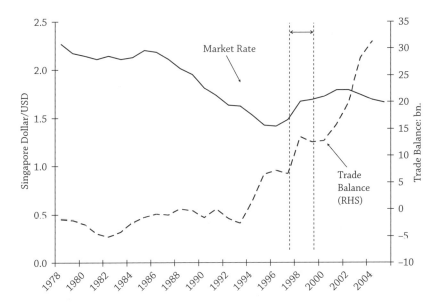

Figure 7.7.
Singapore: Trade Balance and Exchange Rate

For the most part, the existing literature that studies the impact of the exchange rate on trade balances has largely concentrated on debtor economies depreciating against the U.S. dollar. Many more examples can be found where a debtor country reduces its trade deficit by depreciating its currency either voluntarily or involuntarily in a crisis. Due to apparently significant improvements in trade balances in these countries, researchers tend to conclude that a shift in exchange rate certainly should be followed by a trade balance correction. Hence they deduce that if depreciation improves the trade balance, the converse should be true too. Enhanced by predictions of elasticity models for debtor economies, currency appreciations are widely (but incorrectly as we shall show) believed to reduce trade surpluses.

However, we will attest below that this is not necessarily the case. Even though currency depreciation followed by trade balance improvement has been commonplace, an appreciation will not necessarily induce a reduction in a creditor country's trade surplus.

THE UNITED STATES IS DIFFERENT

Due to the asymmetry of the dollar standard, we cannot simply flip the signs and call them the impact effects on the United States. First, exchange rate depreciation of a debtor country often does not have any major impacts on U.S. price level or even price changes, because the latter is determined by the U.S. output level (equation 23). Second, there is no wealth effect from currency revaluation that will change overall consumption (equation 20).

Consequently, what we observe in the United States, dollar appreciation is mainly reflected in falling domestic investment and not in changes in its price level or consumption. Since the dollar is more expensive now relative to the debtor economy's currency, it is more economic to invest in the debtor economy than in the United States. Furthermore, domestic investment in the United States drops and domestic absorption also decreases (equation 20). At the same time, the overall output growth slows down as a result of dollar appreciation, leaving the trade balance with an indeterminate sign. This is equivalent to saying even though U.S. exports may slow down, its imports can be set back as well. Obversely, a depreciation of the dollar has an ambiguous effect on the U.S. trade balance in the short run. In the long run, exchange rate changes just wash out.

CREDITOR COUNTRY'S APPRECIATION AGAINST THE DOLLAR

After the end of the Asian Financial Crisis in 1998, most East Asian economies switched from trade deficits to trade surpluses. As they paid off the foreign debts incurred previously, some of them also emerged as net creditor economies. Because of their trade surpluses, these economies are often under pressure to appreciate their currencies no matter whether they maintain a free-float or dollar peg (soft or hard) as their exchange rate policy. However, does currency appreciation necessarily help them reduce trade surpluses and U.S. trade deficits? The following analysis gives a negative answer.

Suppose in a creditor economy a discrete appreciation of its exchange rate takes place. In the short run, domestic prices begin to fall (equation 14). Output also slows down because of currency appreciation ($e\downarrow$) and the monetary tightening effect following such appreciation. Consumption is cut back because of the output slowdown and the negative wealth effect: the domestic currency price of foreign dollar wealth also falls (equation 16). Appreciation also increases the real interest rate ($i - \dot{p}$)↑ and makes investment goods more expensive. Hence domestic investment is also set back (equation 16), reinforcing a decrease of overall domestic absorption ($C + I + G$). In the end, since both output and domestic absorption decrease, the net impact on the trade balance is ambiguous.

This result can be easily verified by the Japanese experience since the 1980s. As Japan was arm-twisted to appreciate yen from 360 in 1971 to below 100 in 1995, the Japanese trade surplus with the United States did not narrow at all. Even in the short run, Japanese imports did not respond to yen appreciation as predicted by the elasticities models. (See table 7.4 and figure 7.8.)

Empirically, there are fewer examples of creditor countries being forced to appreciate. First, let's take a look of Japan. Figure 7.8 illustrates the trade balance, imports, exports, and yen-dollar

Table 7.4. CREDITOR'S APPRECIATION AGAINST DOLLAR

	Wealth Effect	Investment Effect	Domestic Absorption	Import	Export	Trade Balance
Creditor	↓	↓	↓	↓	↓	?
U.S.	-	↑	↑	↑	↑	?
Rest of world						?

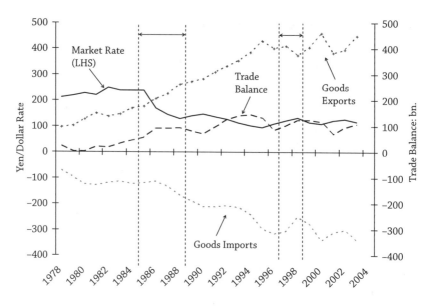

Figure 7.8.
Japanese Trade Balance, Imports, Exports, and Exchange Rate

exchange rate on a bi-axis chart. During the period succeeding the Plaza Accord, Japanese yen appreciated from 250 yen to a dollar in 1985 to 130 yen to a dollar in 1989. However, the Japanese trade surplus continued to grow. Ever since the 1970s, yen appreciations have been unable to "correct" the Japan-U.S. trade imbalance, and Japan has kept posting a large trade surplus versus the United States—as shown by figure 7.8.

Second, consider China. Figure 7.9 shows that the RMB appreciated against the dollar from 8.62 yuan per dollar to 8.31 yuan per dollar between 1994 and 1996, while the Sino-U.S. trade surplus more than doubled. From July 2005 to January 2007, the renminbi appreciated moderately from 8.28 yuan per dollar to 7.7 yuan per dollar, and the trade surplus doubled again (figure 7.9). Clearly something else is going on in China's economy that cannot be explained by the exchange rate.

Due to the asymmetry, we should also examine the impact effects on the United States. The dollar depreciates against the creditor economy's currency, but any price change in the United

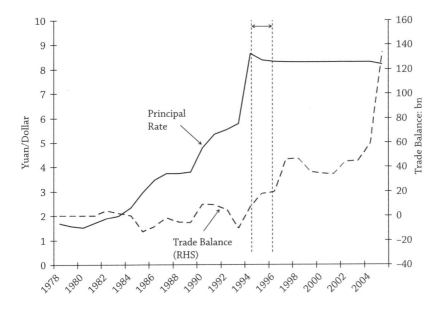

Figure 7.9.
China: Trade Balance and Exchange Rate

States is minimal. Output increases as a result of undervaluation. Domestic absorption also grows because the United States becomes a relatively cheaper place in which to invest. Consequently, the U.S. current-account deficit may increase or decrease in the short run. In the long run, this dollar depreciation will not change the level of output, domestic absorption, trade surplus, or prices.

SPECIAL ANALYSIS OF EAST ASIA

With the asymmetry brought by the dollar standard taken into consideration, our analysis of open economies implies that the effects on the trade balance brought about by exchange rate changes are complex. In most cases, we still cannot predict how the balance of trade will move, except for the case of debtor country after depreciation. However, that this is the only predictable case creates little excitement because of the harmful consequences for economic growth and the financial sector in the debtor economy whose currency depreciates. Yet we would like to further analyze the consequences of fluctuations in the yen/dollar rate for other East Asian economies that are more or less pegged to the dollar.

Impact of Fluctuations in the Yen-Dollar Rate on a Smaller Asian Country Pegged to the Dollar

In East Asia in particular, a third country may also be affected when the yen-dollar rate fluctuates. According to McKinnon (2005, ch. 2), East Asian economies have synchronized business cycles that are related to fluctuations of the yen against the dollar. When the yen is high, East Asian economies other than Japan enjoy high investment and consumption growth; when the yen is low, these other economies have a slower pace of business.

Because most East Asian economies are soft dollar peggers, when the yen appreciates against the dollar, it also appreciates against other major East Asian currencies. A higher yen implies it is more expensive to invest in Japan domestically and therefore Japanese outward FDI (foreign direct investment) increases, with much of it going to other East Asian countries. Therefore economies such as Hong Kong, Indonesia, Korea, Malaysia, Philippines, Singapore, and Thailand all enjoy a stimulus during yen appreciations but suffer from a slowdown during yen depreciations (table 7.5). During good times, both imports and exports grow rapidly, whereas the net trade effect is ambiguous.

Crisis: An Asian Debtor Economy Depreciates against the Dollar Reinforced by a Depreciation of the Yen

During the East Asian financial crisis, the five crisis economies were dollar debtors. They suffered from the direct impacts of

Table 7.5. THE IMPACT OF FLUCTUATIONS IN THE YEN-DOLLAR RATE ON A
SMALLER ASIAN COUNTRY PEGGED TO DOLLAR

	Wealth Effect	Investment Effect	Indirect Investment	Domestic Absorption	Import	Export	Trade Balance
Yen appreciates	-	-	↑	↑	↑	↑	?
Yen depreciates	-	-	↓	↓	↓	↓	?

currency depreciations against the dollar as well as indirectly from yen depreciation against the dollar. The yen fell from 80 to the dollar in April 1995 to reach 147 to the dollar in March 1998, thus increasing the destructive impact of the great crisis (table 7.6). Even though export goods appeared to be cheaper and exports may have grown faster than before, the significant reduction in domestic absorption and output was catastrophic. First, domestic direct investment from Japan in the five crisis economies slumped because of the weakening yen. This magnified the depressing effect of their defaults on dollar debts. This largely tempered the direct and indirect investment effect of the depreciation. Due to fears of collapse of the five crisis economies, investors chose not to further invest, even though devaluation made investment relatively cheaper. As the yen dropped against the dollar, Japanese investors also had more incentives to stay within Japan. Because foreign exchange indebtedness became more onerous in East Asian debtor countries, consumption also slumped from this negative wealth effect. Therefore, domestic absorption decreased faster than output slowed, and each of the five countries' trade balances rapidly improved.

Like other crisis economies suffering from foreign debts and forced to depreciate their currencies, East Asian crisis economies all had trade balance improvements, as shown in figures 7.2–7.7. Because of the collapse of their financial sectors during the crisis, and the indirect investment effect, investment and consumption in the crisis countries slumped.

Table 7.6. CRISIS FOR AN ASIAN DEBTOR ECONOMY DEPRECIATING AGAINST THE DOLLAR REINFORCED BY A DEPRECIATION OF THE YEN

	Wealth Effect	Investment Effect	Indirect Investment	Domestic Absorption	Import	Export	Trade Balance
Debtor	↓↓	?	?	↓↓	↓↓	↑	↑↑
U.S.	-	↓	-	↓	↓	↓	?
Rest of world							↓

Barro (2001) charted investment ratios for these countries between 1960 and 2000.[2] According to his records, Indonesia, Malaysia, South Korea, and Thailand all had dramatic declines in investment in 1998, and it took a long time for them to recover. The investment lapse in Philippines was relatively smaller but it was probably related to the fact that the investment ratio in Philippines had been low historically. This substantiates our argument that the trade balance improvement during the East Asian crisis was mainly caused by the fall in domestic absorption.

CONCLUSIONS

This chapter discusses the ex post impact of a discrete exchange rate change and its implications for the net trade balance. We emphasized the difference between dollar debtor and dollar creditor countries and concluded that even though currency devaluation may improve the trade balance of a debtor country, appreciation may or may not reduce the surplus of a creditor country. It is therefore inappropriate to follow the elasticity model for using the exchange rate to adjust trade balance predictably when the wealth effect, investment effect, and indirect investment effect (in East Asia) are all considered.

On July 21, 2005, China shifted its decade-long currency peg to the dollar by 2.1 percent. Although it was a baby step, we deem it as a symbolic move in China's exchange rate regime—and indeed was followed by other small appreciations. Our model attests that such moves may not induce a reduction in China's trade surplus. Indeed, empirical evidence shows that China's trade surplus remained large for several years after that. Even in 2012, China is still subject to foreign political pressure to appreciate its currency on the mistaken belief that this will reduce its trade surplus.

Unfortunately, the expectation of renminbi appreciation invites massive hot money inflows to speculate on further appreciations, making the problem of domestic monetary control much more difficult. As suggested in McKinnon and Ohno (1997), China could follow Japan's steps into deflation and even a zero-interest liquidity trap if it continues to appreciate. Only time will tell.

NOTES

1. This is a very strong assumption. However, relaxing it will not significantly change the implications from our model. U.S. claims on foreigners are generally less liquid, and wealth effects from exchange rate changes are less pronounced.

   Studies have shown that a large proportion of U.S. foreign assets is stored in dollars. According to Gourinchas and Rey (2005), almost all U.S. foreign liabilities are in dollars, but only about 70 percent of U.S. foreign assets are in foreign currencies, such as euro and sterling, instead of the currencies from major trading partners. Consequently, this asymmetry causes a valuation effect on the U.S. trade balance—dollar depreciation should generate positive wealth transfers into the United States and therefore allow trade deficits to persist for longer without a crisis. Using data from 1952 to 2004, Gourinchas and Rey estimate that a 10 percent fall in the dollar transfers about 5 percent of U.S. national income from the rest of the world to the United States. This stabilizing valuation effect, which is independent of the exchange rate impact, is claimed to have contributed as much as 31 percent of the external adjustment.

2. Investment ratio is defined as the ratio of real investment (sum of private and public) to real GDP.

CHAPTER 8

◦◡◦

Why Exchange Rate Changes Will Not Correct Global Trade Imbalances

Nobody disputes that almost three decades of U.S. trade (net saving) deficits have made the global system of finance and trade more accident-prone. Outstanding dollar debts have become huge, and threaten America's own financial future. Insofar as the principal creditor countries in Asia (Japan in the 1980s and 1990s, China since 2000) are industrial countries relying heavily on exports of manufactures, the transfer of their surplus savings to the saving-deficient United States requires that they collectively run large trade surpluses in manufactures. The resulting large American trade deficits have worsened the "natural" decline in the relative size of the American manufacturing sector, and eroded the U.S. industrial base—as shown in chapter 6.

One unfortunate consequence of this industrial decline has been an outbreak of protectionism in the United States, which is exacerbated by the conviction that foreigners have somehow been cheating with their exchange rate and other commercial policies. The most prominent of these have been associated with New York's Senator Charles Schumer. In March 2005, he cosponsored a bill to impose a 27.5 percent tariff on all U.S. imports from China until the renminbi was appreciated. His bill was withdrawn in October

2006, when shown to be obviously incompatible with America's obligations under the World Trade Organization. But Schumer has threatened to craft a new China bill that is WTO compatible.

Furthermore, congressional legislation requires the Secretary of the Treasury to investigate any country that runs a trade surplus with the United States and to pronounce on whether or not the surplus country is manipulating its exchange rate. The current secretary—Timothy Geithner—has narrowly avoiding having to label China a "currency manipulator," which would involve as yet unspecified sanctions that could lead to a trade war.

However, the common idea that a country's exchange rate could, and indeed should, be used to bring its external trade into better balance is often wrong. As shown in chapter 7, this prevailing wisdom is based on faulty economic theorizing. It need not apply in a globalized financial system where capital flows freely internationally. Under financial globalization, forcing a creditor country such as China to appreciate its currency is neither necessary nor sufficient—and need not be even helpful—for reducing its trade surplus.

In chapter 7, Helen Qiao developed a complete macroeconomic model that showed the trade surplus of a creditor country need not fall when its currency appreciated and the investment decision is "globalized," that is, is sensitive to the exchange rate. Here I present the same result more succinctly but in the context of a much less complete macroeconomic model. What are the issues involved?

THE EXCHANGE RATE AND THE TRADE
BALANCE: THE DEBATE

For a "home" country, consider the identity from the national income accounts:

$$X - M = S - I = \text{Trade (Saving) Surplus,}$$

where X is exports and M is imports (both broadly defined), and S is gross national saving and I is gross domestic investment.

Most economists and commentators focus just on the left-hand side of this accounting identity. It suggests that a depreciation of the home currency will make exports cheaper in world markets, and they will expand. Similarly, the home country's imports will become more expensive in domestic currency, so they should contract. Thus conventional wisdom has it that the overall trade balance should improve if the underlying price elasticities for exporting and importing are even moderately high. This seemingly plausible result is very intuitive, so even journalists can understand and perpetuate it.

But this elasticities approach is basically microeconomic and quite deceptive. The export function X is looked at on its own—and the demand for imports M is looked at on its own—even by supposedly sophisticated econometricians who purport to measure separately the price elasticities of exports, and of imports, to exchange rate changes. Thus it is called the elasticities approach to the trade balance.

However, if you analyze the right-hand side $(S - I)$ of the identity, the emphasis is macroeconomic. For the trade balance to improve with exchange depreciation, overall domestic expenditures must fall relative to aggregate output. This is the same as saying that domestic saving must rise relative to domestic investment. Looking at it this way, one cannot presume that U.S. net saving will rise when the dollar is devalued.

Indeed, the presumption may go the other way when domestic investment (fueled in part by multinational firms) is sensitive to the exchange rate. Suppose the RMB were to appreciate sharply against the dollar. Potential investors—either foreign or domestic, would now see China as a more expensive place in which to invest and the United States less expensive. This might set off a minor investment boom in the United States, where investment expenditures rise from a relatively small base, and a major slump in China's huge investment sector—which is currently about 45 percent of GNP. Overall, investment-led expenditures in China would fall, the economy would contract, and Chinese imports could fall.

This is what happened to Japan from the 1980s into the mid-1990s when the yen went ever higher. Japan became a higher-cost place in which to invest, so that large Japanese firms decamped to invest in lower-cost Asian countries, and in the United States itself. Even though yen appreciation slowed Japan's export growth, the trade surplus of the slumping economy increased (ch. 7).

No wonder China is reluctant to appreciate! Like Japan in the 1980s and 1990s, its trade (saving) surplus would likely not diminish because domestic saving is relatively insensitive to the exchange rate even though investment in a globalized financial-industrial world is sensitive. However, foreign critics in the United States and Europe with the misleading elasticities model (which doesn't take international investment choices into account) in their heads, would come back and say, "You just didn't appreciate enough." With this adverse expectation of continual RMB appreciation, the upshot would be further hot money inflows. The People's Bank of China would be, as has been described in chapter 5, forced to intervene to buy dollars on a grand scale to prevent an indefinite upward spiral in the RMB. But the accumulation of dollar foreign exchange reserves threatens a loss of internal monetary control and inflation as base money in China's banking system expands from the foreign exchange intervention—and cannot be completely sterilized. China's monetary control problem is exacerbated by American China bashing on the exchange rate.

So "exogenous" exchange rate changes without planned absorption adjustment are quite ambiguous in their effect on the net trade (saving) balance of an open economy. But suppose we get the necessary changes in absorption adjustment that is properly two-sided: the deficit country raises taxes or otherwise cuts expenditures, and vice versa for the surplus country. In chapter 9, I show that such changes would be sufficient to correct the trade imbalance without invoking any need to change the exchange rate. That is, the dollar need not (best not) be depreciated for the U.S. trade deficit to be reduced.

CHAPTER 9

◌◦◌

The Transfer Problem in Reducing the U.S. Current-Account Deficit

In this chapter I argue that correcting global trade imbalances is a form of the transfer problem: spending must be transferred from trade-deficit countries (mainly the United States) to trade-surplus countries. Reducing the U.S. current-account deficit requires that net saving, that is, saving minus investment, be increased in the United States and reduced abroad—particularly in Asia. But contrary to most literature on the subject, exchange rates need not, and probably best not, be changed as part of the transfer process for improving the U.S. trade balance. To show why this is so, I draw on the older literature on the transfer problem associated with paying war reparations. Adjustment in absorption, that is, aggregate spending, is two-sided because the loser (the transferor) must raise taxes to pay an indemnity to the winner (the transferee), which then spends it. But there is no presumption that the terms of trade must turn against the transferor. That is, the losing country, which is forced into running a trade surplus (or smaller deficit), need not depreciate its real exchange rate to effect the transfer.

Like it or not, the dollar is at the center of the world's monetary system, while simultaneously the United States runs large current account and trade deficits. As shown in chapter 6, the United States couldn't have run such deficits for more than three decades if the dollar were not the definitive international money. Because much of the world is on a dollar standard, only the United States can borrow abroad indefinitely in terms of its *own* currency to cover its relatively low level of saving. This is possible as long as the U.S. Federal Reserve Bank keeps the purchasing power of the dollar fairly stable so that countries with trade surpluses are loath to appreciate against the currency in which most of world trade is invoiced. Thus, there is no immediate crisis and no need for precipitate action by governments—particularly on the exchange rate front—to "correct" the U.S. current-account deficit.

Nevertheless this continual U.S. borrowing is *unsatisfactory* even if *sustainable*. The world is treated to the spectacle of its richest economy grabbing the lion's share of international finance that would be potentially available for economic development in much poorer countries. In addition, the process of transferring resources from the rest of the world creates tensions within the American economy itself.

What is the transfer mechanism? In order to transfer real resources from the rest of the world (apart from surplus-saving oil-producing emirates), the United States runs very large trade deficits in manufactures from surplus-saving industrial economies such as China, Japan, a host of smaller ones in East Asia, and Germany. This real transfer of manufactures needed to cover the shortfall in American saving speeds the contraction in employment in U.S. manufacturing (ch. 6) beyond the natural rate of decline experienced by other mature industrial economies.

The upshot is a protectionist backlash in the United States, particularly by members of Congress with manufacturing constituencies. Instead of blaming America's own deficient saving, which makes foreign borrowing necessary, American politicians incorrectly blame "unfair" foreign trading practices—undervalued currencies, substandard labor practices, dumping of subsidized exports in American markets, and so on. Rather than any imminent collapse in America's credit line with the rest of the world, this protectionist backlash is the serious threat to the world economy.

However, contrary to a widely held belief within the economics profession, devaluing the dollar is itself no panacea for correcting the savings (trade) imbalances across countries. In chapter 7, Hong (Helen) Qiao shows formally that having creditor countries like Japan earlier or China today appreciate the yen or renminbi against the dollar would have no predictable effect on their trade surpluses—unlike what the old and familiar elasticities model of the balance of trade would suggest. In effect, their savings surpluses (or the American saving deficiency) need not be corrected if the dollar is devalued. Nevertheless, any such major change in the dollar's nominal exchange rate could create serious monetary imbalances in the world economy: deflation in the appreciating countries or inflation in the United States, with the trade-off between the two being somewhat arbitrary (McKinnon 2005), but where any long-run impact on the "real" exchange rate washes out.

Instead, correcting international trade imbalances must start with countries' changing domestic absorption, that is, aggregate spending, relative to income. International adjustment requires that net saving be increased in the United States or reduced abroad—particularly in East Asia. To be effective in reducing the trade imbalance, absorption adjustment must be two-sided—and if it were so, would itself be sufficient to right the trade imbalance between, say, China and the United States. No additional or "supporting" exchange rate changes would be necessary or even helpful.

So in building a more formal model to show this, let us suppose that absorption adjustment is balanced and two-sided. That is, taxes fall abroad as they increase in the United States. Unfortunately, modeling possible monetary-cum-price-level repercussions together with the transfer itself presents problems. Instead, I will follow the time-honored but treacherous tradition in international economics of separating out monetary issues from "real" ones.

THE TRANSFER PROBLEM

The transfer problem is first modeled in real terms. To emphasize the importance of two-sided adjustment, I utilize the older literature on the economics of war reparations. The loser must raise taxes to pay a fixed sum to the winner, who then spends it and increases his absorption by that amount. What then happens endogenously to the real exchange rate?

To reduce the U.S. current-account deficit from, say, 6.5 to 3.5 percent of GDP, adjustment must start with a permanent fall in total U.S. absorption relative to income of at least 3 percent— and with complementary inverse changes abroad. Because the United States bulks so large in the world economy, complementary foreign reactions to any change in American spending behavior must be explicitly modeled.

Consider the accounting identity

$$Y - A = CA = -CA^* = A^* - Y^*,$$

where A is U.S. domestic absorption (total spending), Y is output (GDP), CA is the current-account surplus (negative in the American case), and the starred variables are the counterparts in rest of the world (ROW).

Given full employment output at home and abroad, then clearly CA can only improve if $\Delta A < 0$, $\Delta A^* > 0$, and $\Delta A = -\Delta A^*$. To correct a trade imbalance for a large country like the United States, *absorption adjustment must be symmetric with ROW*.

Let us assume that the 3 percent U.S. decline in absorption is not abrupt, but nevertheless is fairly definite as part of corrective government program. That is, fiscal improvement is highly visible and the Federal Reserve Bank avoids future episodes of excessively easy money that unduly stimulate U.S. private spending—as with the ultralow interest rate policy of 2003–04, which created the U.S. housing bubble of 2005–08.

If well signaled and spread out over some years, the fall in absorption itself would gradually bid down the price of U.S. nontradables relative to tradables—which remain buoyed by robust external demand. This natural fall in the relative price of nontradables—largely services of all kinds—with slower wage growth in that sector gradually releases capital and labor for greater U.S. production of both importables and exportables. Of course nobody (least of all economists!) would know exactly how much the relative prices of nontradables would eventually fall in the United States or increase abroad. But the American economy is flexible, with workers and firms continually adjusting to various shocks, and a 3 percent fall in absorption over some years isn't all that large. In the modern world, where the distinction between tradables and nontradables is eroding, the necessary relative price changes would be quite modest in the long run.

However, absorption adjustment must be two-sided, if only because of the accounting identity: the gradual fall in U.S. absorption relative to income must be matched by a gradual rise in foreign absorption relative to income. Otherwise, unilateral absorption adjustment by either side to right the trade imbalance will always be frustrated. Putting pressure on China and Japan to increase consumption is all well and good, but only if matched by a reduction in consumption in the United States.

Suppose both sides begin the necessary adjustment—reducing absorption in the United States and raising it abroad. In long-run equilibrium, we know that relative prices of nontradables will fall in the United States and increase abroad. But should one presume that the U.S. terms of trade, the price of American exports relative to American imports, need fall as the U.S. trade deficit declines? Essentially, and perhaps surprisingly to most economists, the answer is no. In the long run, any change in America's real exchange rate as measured by its terms of trade would likely be small with an unpredictable sign.

When one speaks of the *real* exchange rate, economists use at least two definitions.

The first and most common definition is simply the terms of trade, and it arises naturally out of the old elasticities model. In its most stripped-down, short-run version, the elasticities model presumes that the domestic-currency price of each country's export good is fixed. Thus a devaluation of the home currency reduces its terms of trade one-for-one—and this relative price effect is the mechanism by which it is presumed that exports expand and imports contract to improve the trade balance. This assumption is often incorporated into large-scale macroeconometric models (such as the Sigma model used by the U.S. Federal Reserve) by assuming all trading partners effectively produce just one aggregate good, some of which is exported and the rest consumed at home. Then, again, real exchange rate changes are associated with changes in the terms of trade.

An alternative definition of the "real" exchange rate is the price of tradable goods collectively relative to nontradables collectively. A real devaluation would then be defined as an increase in the relative price of tradables. And as we have just seen, it is variation in this relative price that is most relevant for the transfer problem—with the relative price of tradables rising in the transferor and falling in the transferee. But to facilitate the transfer, does this leave any room for changes in the terms of trade?

THE JONES MODEL AND THE TERMS OF TRADE

From the 1950s into the 1970s, there was a spirited "real" (nonmonetary) literature on the transfer problem associated with war reparations. Given a fall in spending in the home country (the loser and the transferor) and a rise in spending in the foreign country (the winner and the transferee), what would happen to the terms of trade? The orthodox presumption then as now was that there would be a secondary burden on the home country as its terms of trade deteriorated: the price of its exportables would fall relative to its importables in order for its trade balance to improve. However, several eminent authors—Paul Samuelson, Harry Johnson, John Chipman, and Ronald Jones—with some heavy mathematical artillery, in the context of a long-run real model where resources remained fully employed, successfully questioned the validity of the orthodox presumption that a real devaluation was necessary.

In particular, Ronald Jones in his article "Presumption and the Transfer Problem" (1975) built a model with a nontradable and two tradables sectors (importables and exportables) in each country. He showed that the relative price of nontradables declines in the transferor, and rises in the transferee, but what happened to the terms of trade is quite ambiguous. Only by making extremely strong assumptions about specialization in production or consumption could Jones get either the orthodox or the antiorthodox presumption of the change in the terms of trade to hold. However, for any large economy such as the United States with well-diversified production and consumption, the effect of a transfer on its terms of trade is ambiguous—and presumably a second-order effect compared to the primary changes in the prices of nontradables relative to tradables at home and abroad.

We can extract Jones's main result thus. In a stable market, the terms of trade of the transferor (the home country) worsen if and only if:

$$m_2^* + \omega^* m_3^* > m_2 + \omega m_3.$$

Commodity 2 is the home country's importable and foreign country's exportable. Commodity 3 is the nontraded good in each country; m_j is the marginal propensity to consume commodity j at home, and m_j^* the marginal propensity to consume j abroad.

(The subscripts *i* or *j* can assume the values 1, 2, or 3, in Jones's model.) The ω^* and ω terms are positive parameters, embodying the substitution effects in consumption and production triggered by the transfer's alteration of the relative price of nontradables to tradables in each country. If $\omega \approx \omega^*$, then terms of trade turn against the transferor only if $m_2^* > m_2$. That is, the foreign country (transferee) has a higher propensity to consume its own export good than the home country's (transferor) propensity to consume imports. In countries with large nontradables sectors, there is no reason to believe a priori that such a condition holds.

One can get an intuitive sense of Jones's result by noting that as absorption falls in the transferor, and the relative price of its nontradables begin to decline, then its exports will increase and imports decline as resources move into its tradables sector. If, myopically, one stopped at this point with adjustment only in the transferor, it then seems as if the orthodox presumption holds: the price of its exports would be bid down relative to the price of imports.

However, absorption adjustment must be two-sided. As the transferee's absorption of both tradables and nontradables increases, its nontradable prices are bid up relatively so that resources are drawn out of its tradable sectors. The transferee's exports will tend to fall and imports from the transferor rise. This foreign pressure by itself would tend to raise the prices of the transferor's exports relative to its imports. So putting the two offsetting sides together, Jones showed that there is *no presumption* as to which way the transferor's terms of trade will move. If we use the terms-of-trade (most common) definition of the "real" exchange rate, there is no presumption as to which direction, if any, the real exchange rate need move to facilitate the transfer in the long run. And in the short run, when export prices are "sticky" in each country's home currency, there is no presumption as to which way the nominal exchange rate should change either.

What are the lessons from this "real" long-run model of the transfer problem?

1. Balanced international adjustment in both transferor and transferee is important for preventing a secondary burden on the transferor of having the terms of trade turn against it as its trade balance improves, and for maintaining macroeconomic equilibrium in the (two-country) system as a whole.
2. Precipitate action to foment a discrete major "real" depreciation of the dollar—which would initially turn the terms of trade against the transferor, that is, the United States, at the start of the adjustment process—is unwarranted. This would be painful but also quite unnecessary. In the long run, when the U.S. trade deficit was substantially reduced through mutual absorption adjustment, little or no change in the initial real exchange rate need characterize the final equilibrium.

Martin Wolf of the *Financial Times* constructively criticized the preceding analysis and suggested that "the price changes needed to bring that shift [a reduction in the U.S. trade deficit] around may not happen easily under a fixed nominal exchange rate, particularly if it requires a sizeable fall in nominal wages." This is a common Keynesian worry for maintaining aggregate demand should domestic absorption be reduced.

Wolf is right to focus on the nature of wage adjustment. If taxes were gradually raised in the United States and decreased abroad by 3 percent of U.S. GNP, American *after-tax* wages and returns to the other factors of production must fall by 3 percent on average—as would foreign after-tax wages rise by the same amount in dollar terms. This is the necessary primary burden on Americans for reducing the U.S. current deficit.

However, it is not at all clear that average *before-tax* (nominal) wages need fall in the United States. There would be downward pressure on wages in the U.S. nontradables sector but upward pressure in the tradables sector from the increased foreign demand for American exports. The expansion of absorption abroad—most important for maintaining aggregate demand and limiting any necessary fall in American pretax wages—should parallel the contraction in the United States. In particular, there would be no need for a nominal depreciation of the dollar as an inflationary backdoor device for reducing American real (before tax) wages as an adjunct to effecting the transfer.

Dollar depreciation would impose an unnecessary secondary burden on the United States as the terms of trade turned against it in the short run, although any real depreciation would eventually unwind in the long run. Because domestic export prices are sticky in the short run, a stable nominal exchange rate would have the great advantage of keeping the terms of trade fairly constant—rather than fluctuating unpredictably as mutual absorption adjustment proceeded. Without devaluing the dollar, U.S. net exports would gradually increase anyway.

A CONCLUDING NOTE

This chapter has approached the problem of correcting global imbalances from a somewhat unusual angle. The usual approach is to start off by estimating what the necessary "real" devaluation of the dollar must be to reduce the U.S. trade deficit by a predetermined amount—as in Cline (2005), or Obstfeld and Rogoff (2005). However, Qiao (2007 and chapter 7) has shown that appreciations by America's creditor countries, with large overhangs of dollar assets such as those in East Asia, are most unlikely to reduce their trade (saving) surpluses. Moreover, McKinnon (2007b) emphasizes the adverse deflationary consequences of any one of them being forced to appreciate—particularly in the face of continued expectations of further appreciation, as with the ever-higher yen for Japan in the 1970s to the mid-1990s, and the ever-higher renminbi for China today.

Any new international "Plaza" agreement should focus on directly adjusting international savings imbalances and not on exchange rates. Because naked exchange rate changes aimed at correcting international savings imbalances do no good and possibly much harm, the approach taken here has focused more directly on the underlying international transfer problem. Clearly, expenditures (absorption) must fall relative to income in the United States and rise relative to income in countries in East Asia and elsewhere. If governments want to reduce America's trade deficit and Asia's trade surplus, then they must act jointly to coordinate their fiscal and complementary other policies to achieve this result.

PART III

China

Adjusting to the Dollar Standard

CHAPTER 10

☙

High Wage Growth under Stable Dollar Exchange Rates

Japan, 1950–71 and China, 1994–2011

International saving and current-account imbalances aside, suppose a country such as China, with low wages but very high productivity growth, trades with a country such as the United States, with much lower productivity growth but higher real wages. When wages are "sticky," as traditional theory would have it, isn't exchange rate flexibility with ongoing appreciation of the renminbi more or less necessary to balance international competitiveness?

In the high-growth economy, however, wages *are* flexible. When wages grow about 10 to 15 percent per year, first differences are high relative to wage levels. International competitiveness can be roughly balanced in the medium term when high quarterly wage increases match high productivity growth. In the very long run, the level of money wages in the high-growth peripheral country converges to their level in the slower-growing center. But the key is to ensure that monetary and exchange rate conditions are right so that high wage growth accurately reflects productivity gains in the medium term.

In the 1950s and 1960s under the Bretton Woods system of fixed dollar exchange rates, how differential wage growth became the mode of international adjustment was first articulated for high-growth Scandinavia when the Swedish, Norwegian, and Danish currencies were all pegged to the dollar. But very high productivity growth in postwar Japan relative to the United States, when the yen/dollar rate was also convincingly fixed from 1949 to 1971, provided an equally striking example of what is now known as the Scandinavian model (SM) of wage adjustment (Lindbeck 1979). When the high-growth country's dollar exchange rate is credibly fixed, the SM has four key features:

1. Purchasing power parity holds: inflation in tradable goods prices converges to that in the center country, in whose currency most world trade is invoiced.
2. Productivity growth in tradable (exportable) manufactures is higher than in the rest of the high-growth economy.
3. Employers in manufacturing, subject to the fixed exchange rate constraint, naturally bid up wages to fully reflect the higher productivity growth in manufacturing.
4. The high wage growth in manufactures then spreads out into the nontradables sector, especially services, where productivity growth is less, causing prices there to increase: the now classic Balassa-Samuelson effect.

THE JAPANESE CASE

When the yen was fixed at 360 to the dollar from 1950 to 1971 under Bretton Woods, the importance of relative wage adjustment between Japan and the United States was pronounced (table 10.1). In that period, Japan's annual growth in real output was 9.45 percent, while industrial production grew an astonishing 14.6 percent—much like China's more recently. Unsurprisingly, the annual growth in Japan's labor productivity of 8.9 percent was far in excess of America's 2.6 percent. However, the balancing item was that average money wages grew at a robust rate of 10 percent per year in Japan and only 4.5 percent in the United States. In Japan's manufacturing export sector with its extremely high growth in labor productivity, employers bid vigorously for both skilled and unskilled workers—subject to remaining internationally competitive at the fixed exchange rate.

Keeping the yen at 360 per dollar effectively anchored Japan's price level for tradable goods. In the 1950s and 1960s, the Japanese wholesale price index (WPI) rose less than 1 percent per year, whereas the American WPI rose a bit more than 1 percent (table 10.1). Because the bulk of world trade was invoiced in dollars, fixing an exchange rate to the dollar was (is) a stronger anchor for Japan's price level than the size of Japanese bilateral trade with the United States would have suggested.

Figure 10.1 shows the dramatic rise of Japanese money wages relative to American money wages in the 1950s and 1960s with the fixed dollar exchange rate.

Table 10.1. JAPAN AND THE UNITED STATES, 1950–1971, WITH THE YEN FIXED AT 360 PER DOLLAR (AVERAGE ANNUAL PERCENTAGE CHANGE IN KEY INDICATORS)

Wholesale prices		Money wages		Consumer prices		Industrial production	
U.S.	Japan	U.S.	Japan	U.S.	Japan	U.S.	Japan
1.63	0.69[a]	4.52	10.00	2.53	5.01	4.40	14.56
Real GDP		**Nominal GDP**		**Narrow money**		**Labor productivity**	
U.S.	Japan	U.S.	Japan	U.S.	Japan	U.S.	Japan
3.84	9.45[a]	6.79	14.52[a]	3.94	16.10[b]	2.55	8.92[c]

[a] 1952–71.
[b] 1953–71.
[c] 1951–71.

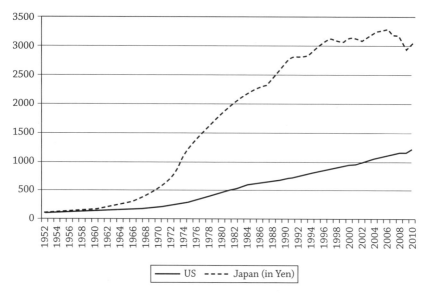

Figure 10.1.
Percentage differences in Manufacturing Wage Growth for the United States and Japan,
1952–2010 (1952 = 100)
Source: Japan Statistics Bureau and Bureau of Labor Statistics

But what happens to wage growth when the national currency is expected to appreciate against that of the center country? After the Nixon shock of 1971, and then continual American pressure to have the yen appreciate further, employers began to expect that yen appreciation would continue so that the high wage growth in Japan tailed off sharply about 1975–77. Japanese wage growth became even *less* than that in the United States, despite Japan's productivity growth remaining much higher (figure 10.2).

From the Nixon shock, the yen had appreciated 17 percent by the end of 1971. Initially, markets treated this discrete appreciation as just a one-time adjustment. But when Japan's trade surplus failed to decline (chs. 7 and 8), the Americans continued to pressure Japan to appreciate the yen—so-called Japan bashing—expectations changed. Reinforced by the Carter shock beginning in 1976 and further yen appreciation, the expectation of an ever-higher yen took hold (McKinnon and Ohno 1997).

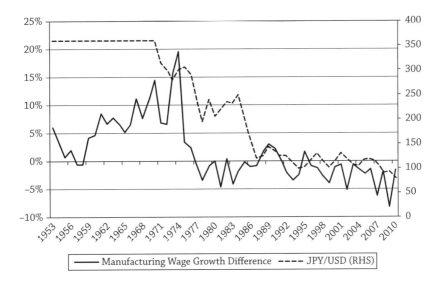

Figure 10.2.
CPI Inflation and Wage Differential between Japan and the United States, and Yen/Dollar
Rate, 1953–2010
Source: Japan Statistics Bureau and Bureau of Labor Statistics

Indeed, the yen rose all the way from 360 to the dollar in early 1971 to touch 80 to the dollar in April 1995.

By the mid-1970s, the expectation of chronic yen appreciation affected wage setting in Japanese labor markets. Employers, particularly exporters in Japan's large manufacturing sector, became more loath to grant generous wage settlements reflecting Japan's higher productivity growth because they could go bankrupt if the yen suddenly ratcheted up in the next period. So employers became much more conservative in wage setting as the yen rose in the foreign exchange markets. This slower growth in wages (relative to productivity growth) added to the deflationary pressure in Japan—particularly after the Plaza Hotel accord of 1985, where a large further appreciation of the yen was negotiated (figure 10.2) and Japanese wholesale prices fell sharply.

This general deflation in Japan continues to the present day, when wage settlements in Japanese industry are still less than those negotiated by their American counterparts. From the principle of open interest parity, this syndrome of the ever-higher yen was also responsible for driving Japanese interest rates close to zero by the mid-1990s. One could then argue that ultralow interest rates in Japan, combined with a sense of triumphalism from the yen going ever higher (we can now buy up the rest of the world!) created huge asset bubbles in both real estate and the stock market in the 1980s. After the bursting of the bubble economy in 1991, the yen continued to rise until April 1995. So the double whammy of imploding asset prices and an overvalued yen knocked Japan off its high growth path. Since then, the economy has suffered two lost decades of little or no real growth with ongoing deflationary pressure (McKinnon 2007b). China beware!

THE CHINESE CASE

After unifying its currency (eliminating multiple exchange rates) and moving to de facto current-account convertibility in 1994, China kept its exchange rate stable at 8.28 yuan per dollar until July 2005. Figure 10.3 shows China's inflation (measured by its CPI) to be high in 1994–96, and, after 1998, to converge close to that in the United States: *equilibrium* in the sense of relative purchasing power parity. But how well did this fixed exchange rate policy anchor China's macroeconomy more generally? Coupled with greater economic openness since the mid-1990s, it helped end the "roller coaster" ride in China's domestic inflation and GDP growth characteristic of the 1980s and early 1990s (figure 10.4), and as explained in more depth in chapter 12.

But more was involved than just stabilizing inflation at a low level. Figure 10.4 shows that China's very high growth in real GDP also became more stable after 1996 to 2010. No doubt other explanations of the end of China's roller-coaster ride in both inflation and real growth rates before 1995 are possible. However, the data are consistent with my hypothesis that fixing the nominal exchange rate provided a much-needed nominal anchor when very rapid financial transformation made purely domestic

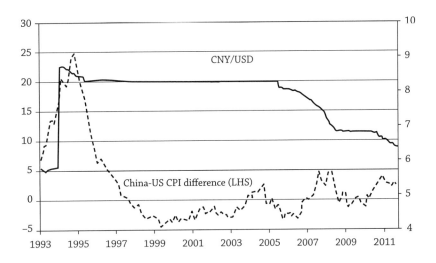

Figure 10.3.
China-U.S. Inflation Differential and Exchange Rate, 1993–2011
Source: IMF

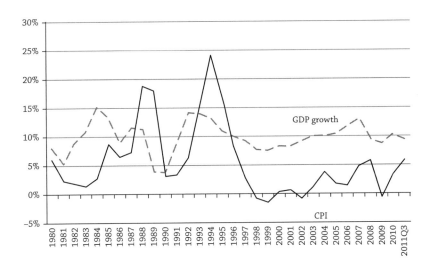

Figure 10.4.
Inflation Rate and Real Growth Rate of China, 1980–2011
Source: IMF

monetary control mechanisms difficult to implement—as was also true of Japan in the 1950s and 1960s.

But to preserve the exchange rate anchor, China's money wages had to grow in line with its rapid productivity growth. From 1995 through 2010 money wages in manufacturing in China increased by 10.4 percent per year and by just 2.5 percent in the United States (see table 10.2). Subsequent evidence for 2011 and 2012 shows Chinese wages growing closer to 15 or 20 percent per year. This wage growth differential approximately reflected the differential growth of labor productivity: about 15 percent in China versus 5 percent in the United States over the decade.

Much of this extraordinary growth in Chinese wages reflects the upgrading of skills and greater work experience of the manufacturing labor force. True, at the margin, the wages of unskilled migrant workers have lagged in past years. Many of these seem to be absorbed into construction activities, where average wages show (slightly) slower growth. But with the yuan/dollar rate fixed or just slowly appreciating (figure 10.5), high wage growth in China seems to balance international competitiveness—at least approximately given the highly imperfect data available—as the Scandinavian model would have it.

To be sure, wage growth and is not always perfectly aligned with high, and somewhat variable, productivity growth. Figure 10.6 shows that China's productivity growth exceeded wage growth in

Table 10.2. CHINA AND THE UNITED STATES, 1995–2010, WITH A FAIRLY STABLE YUAN/DOLLAR (AVERAGE ANNUAL PERCENTAGE CHANGE IN KEY INDICATORS)

Producer prices		Money wages		Consumer prices		Industrial production	
U.S.	China	U.S.	China	U.S.	China	U.S.	China
2.81	1.95	2.50	10.41	2.45	2.97	2.03	13.42
Real GDP		Nominal GDP		Narrow money		Labor productivity	
U.S.	China	U.S.	China	U.S.	China	U.S.	China
2.48	9.93	4.61	13.88	3.06	17.49	5.25	15.75

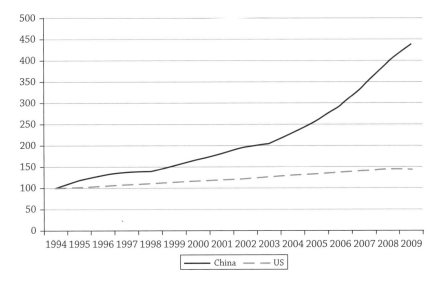

Figure 10.5.
Nominal Manufacturing Wage for the United States and China, 1994–2009 (1994 = 100)

the early 2000s up to about 2005, so that unit labor costs were actually falling. Subsequently, however, wages grew faster than productivity growth—the more so if restated in dollar terms. From July 2005 to July 2008, the RMB appreciated against the dollar about 6 percent per year before it was restabilized for a brief two-year period. Since June 2010 (too recent to be included in the figures), the RMB has again been appreciating gently.

Figure 10.7 tells a similar story in terms of unit labor costs measured wholly in domestic currency, that is, the RMB. From 2001 through 2005, unit labor costs in China fell as domestic productivity growth exceeded wage growth. Since then, manufacturing wages have grown faster than productivity so that manufacturing unit labor costs in China have been rising.

Figure 10.8 shows China's wage growth catching up to productivity growth since 2002 (the base year), and of course growing much faster than in the United States. With the passage of time, it seems as if Chinese wages are on track to converge eventually with those in the United States unless there is some violent

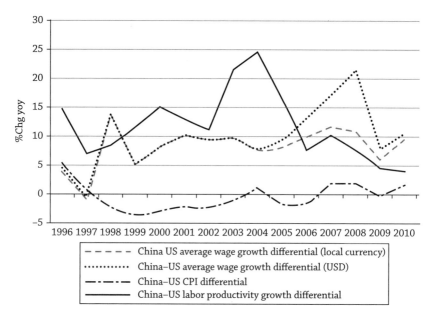

Figure 10.6.
China-U.S. Wage Growth, CPI, and Labor Productivity Growth Differential

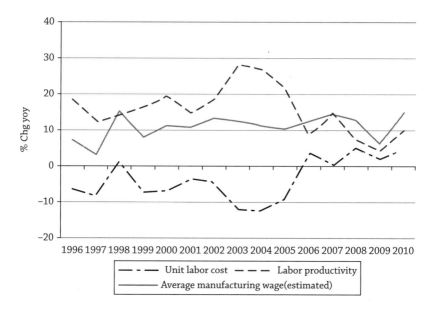

Figure 10.7.
Manufacturing Sector Wage, Labor Productivity, and ULC: Percentage Changes

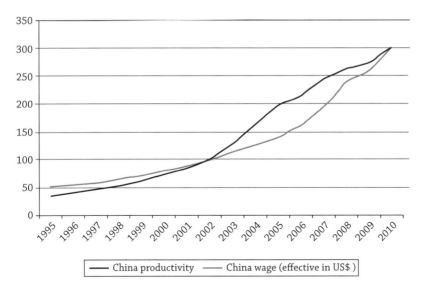

Figure 10.8.
China's Productivity and Wage Growth (2002 = 100)

interruption—such as happened to Japan with the sharp ratcheting up of the yen from the late 1970s into the mid-1990s.

Although this fast rise in Chinese wages better balances international competitiveness, it does not by itself correct the trade imbalance. There remains the need for China to reduce its surplus saving in conjunction with the United States eliminating its saving deficiency—as shown by the analysis in chapters 6 and 9.

THE NEGATIVE RISK PREMIUM IN WAGE GROWTH

Suppose we modify our Scandinavian model of wage determination to introduce the expectation of renminbi appreciation, but the precise amount is uncertain. Because risk-averse employers in export activities don't know how much the renminbi will actually appreciate, they hesitate to bid money wages up by the full amount of expected productivity growth in tradables. A Chinese exporter could go bankrupt if he bid up incremental wages too strongly only to find that the renminbi appreciated more than his mean expectation. Let us call this shortfall in wage growth from employer risk aversion the *negative risk premium* in wage bargaining, WRP < 0. Starting from a position where the domestic price level in China is stable (as was approximately true until the worldwide inflation of 2010–11, as explained in chapter 5), wages increase according to

$$\Delta W = E(\Delta PROD) + E(\Delta S) + WRP,$$

where W is money wages in China, $PROD$ is (real) labor productivity, S is yuan/dollar; Δ is the operator for percentage change, and E is the expectations operator. $E(\Delta S) < 0$ reflects expected appreciation, and $E(\Delta PROD) > 0$ reflects high productivity growth.

If the rate of appreciation was certain, say the renminbi was sure to appreciate by 2.9 percent per year, then $WRP = 0$. Money wages would increase less than productivity growth by 2.9 percentage points. On a balanced deflation path, prices would fall 2.9 per year while real wages grew as much as labor productivity.

But the rate of renminbi appreciation in China is uncertain, so that $WRP < 0$. It is still too soon in 2011 to get any firm estimate of the shortfall in wage increases in China from the uncertainty in exchange appreciation. However, the earlier Japanese experience of massive actual appreciations after 1970, which only later became more or less fully realized, seemed to have first-order impact on Japanese wage growth. Fortunately, the Chinese authorities have been much more resistant to China bashing and, unlike the Japanese experience, there have been no sharp appreciations of the RMB against the dollar—and cumulative appreciation has also been low. In 2012, China has slowed to a halt even gradual appreciation. So China seems to be much less in danger of a sudden, disruptive slowdown in wage growth such as that which afflicted Japan from the 1970s through the mid-1990s (figure 10.2).

A CONCLUDING NOTE

For creditor countries on the periphery of the dollar standard such as China that have current-account (saving) surpluses, mercantile pressure to appreciate their currencies and become more "flexible" is misplaced (as per chapters 7 and 8). Just the expectation of (ongoing) exchange appreciation with high variance seriously disrupts the natural tendency for wage growth to balance productivity growth. It could create a zero-interest liquidity trap in financial markets that leaves the central bank helpless to combat future deflation arising out of actual currency appreciation—as with the earlier experience of Japan (McKinnon and Ohno 1997). Exchange rate appreciation, or the threat of it, causes macroeconomic distress through hot money flows (ch. 5) without having any predictable effect on the trade surpluses of creditor economies (ch. 7). The solution is to credibly fix the central yuan/dollar rate into the indefinite future.

CHAPTER 11

✧

Currency Mismatches on the Dollar's Periphery

Why China as an Immature Creditor Cannot Float Its Exchange Rate

China is again coming under heavy political pressure by the U.S. government, with some foreign officials in Europe and emerging markets chiming in, to appreciate the renminbi. Behind this political clamor is the academic view of many economists that exchange rate "flexibility"[1] is itself desirable—particularly as a way of correcting imbalances in foreign trade. Bowing to this foreign pressure, the People's Bank of China (PBC) announced on June 19, 2010, that it was unhooking its two-year old peg of 6.83 yuan per dollar and would henceforth be more flexible. But since then, the yuan/dollar rate has moved very little. In August 2012 the rate was just 6.36 yuan per dollar, whence the sense of outrage among American and European politicians that they were deceived.

But China's government is trapped in two important respects.

First, government officials and many economists on both sides are in thrall to a false theory: that a discrete appreciation of the RMB against the dollar would have the predictable effect of reducing China's trade surplus and U.S. trade deficit. Once one realizes that China's trade surplus just reflects its net surplus of saving over investment, $S - I$, and vice versa for the saving-deficient United

States, then there is no presumption as to which way $S - I$ would move in either country if the RMB was appreciated. True, an appreciation would reduce China's corporate profitability and some corporate saving. However, in our globalized financial system, investment would fall sharply when China was suddenly seen to be a more expensive country in which to install productive capacity and produce from it. And China's currently extremely high ratio of investment to GDP, about 40 to 45 percent, has a long way to fall. With the greater sensitivity of investment to the exchange rate, any presumption should be that China's trade (net saving surplus) would increase with RMB appreciation (see chapters 7 and 8).

Second, and the major focus of this chapter, is the issue of exchange rate flexibility per se. I will argue that it is impossible for the PBC to withdraw from foreign exchange interventions and let the "market" decide what the rate should be when, at the same time, China has a huge net saving (trade) surplus. That is, floating the yuan/dollar rate is out of the question. Many well-meaning foreign commentators, who are not overtly bashing China to appreciate its currency, still believe that greater market-determined exchange flexibility is warranted. U.S. Treasury secretary Timothy Geithner seems to think so:

> "It is China's decision about what to do with the exchange rate—
> they're a sovereign country," Geithner said. "But I think it is enormously in their interest to move, over time, to let the exchange
> rate reflect market forces, and I am confident that they will do
> what is in their interest," he said while visiting Boeing and other
> exporters in Washington State. (Associated Press, May 23, 2010)

Secretary Geithner's tone here is much more measured and careful than in previous episodes of American China bashing where various congressmen, journalists, industrialists, union officials, and economists have called for a large appreciation of the RMB against the dollar. Nevertheless, Secretary Geithner's more moderate and seemingly reasonable approach to let the yuan/dollar rate reflect "market forces," that is, by floating or otherwise becoming more flexible, is still not feasible. Why?

CHINA AS AN IMMATURE INTERNATIONAL CREDITOR

China is in the historically unusual position of being an *immature* creditor: its own currency, the renminbi, is hardly used at all in financing its huge trade (saving) surplus. Instead the world—particularly the Asian part of it—is still on a dollar standard. The dollar is the invoice currency of choice for most of Chinese exports and imports and for open-market, that is, nongovernment-controlled, financial flows. So we have the anomaly that the world's largest creditor country cannot use its own currency in lending to foreigners.

The lag in the international use of the RMB is partly because China's domestic financial markets are not fully developed: interest rate restrictions as well as residual capital controls on foreign exchange inflows remain. But a more fundamental constraint is that the U.S. dollar has the first-mover advantage of being ensconced as "international money." World financial markets shun the use of more than one or two national currencies for clearing international payments—with the euro now in second place. But the euro's use in payments clearing is still pretty well confined to Europe's own backyard (Eastern Europe and former European colonies). Thus dollar dominance makes the internationalization of the RMB very difficult—although the People's Bank of China is trying hard to encourage the RMB's use in international transacting on China's immediate borders.

The upshot is that China's own currency is still not used much in lending to foreigners. Foreigners won't borrow from Chinese banks in RMB or issue RMB-denominated bonds in Shanghai. (A very small market in RMB-denominated bonds, now called "dim sum" bonds, operates in an offshore market out of Hong Kong.)

But, apart from direct investments abroad by Chinese corporations, private finance for China's trade surplus would have to take the form of Chinese banks, insurance companies, pension funds, and so on, acquiring liquid foreign exchange assets—largely in dollars. But their domestic liabilities—bank deposits and annuity or pension liabilities—are all denominated in RMB. Because of this *currency mismatch*, the exchange rate risks for China's private banks and other financial institutions are simply too great for them to be international financial intermediaries, that is, to lend to foreigners on a large-enough scale.

China's current large trade (saving) surpluses, which run at about $200 to $300 billion per year, would quickly cumulate to become much greater than the combined net worth of all of China's private financial institutions. Because these private (nonstate) institutions would refuse to accept the exchange risk (possible dollar depreciation) of holding dollar assets on a significant scale, the international intermediation of China's saving surplus is left to the central government. The problem is worsened by American "China bashing" to appreciate the RMB, the expectation of which makes foreigners even more loath to borrow in RMB—while stimulating perverse flows of hot money *into* China. The upshot is that China's central government steps in to intermediate and control the country's saving surplus in several different ways.

1. The accumulation of huge liquid official reserves of foreign exchange, currently about $3.2 trillion, in the State Administration of Foreign Exchange (SAFE).
2. The creation of sovereign wealth funds, like the China Investment Corporation (CIC), which invests overseas in bonds, equities, or real estate.
3. Encouraging China's large state-owned enterprises such as SINOPEC to invest in, or partner with, foreign oil companies in exploration and production.

4. Quasi-barter aid and investment programs in developing countries that generate a return flow of industrial materials.[2]

Under 4, China does not give "aid" to African or Latin American countries in the conventional form of liquid dollar deposits. Instead, China's overseas investments are combined with aid under the fairly strict government control of China's Export-Import Bank or the Department of Commerce. In return for using Chinese state-owned construction companies to build large-scale infrastructure for ports, railways, power plants, and so on, the recipient country agrees to repay China by giving it a claim on a future stream of copper or iron ore or oil or whatever mineral that the infrastructure investments make possible, whence the "quasi barter" nature of the deal. Because these foreign-aid/investment projects are under the control of state-owned financial intermediaries, they become effectively *illiquid*: they will not be suddenly sold off and become part of hot money flows back into China.

Each of these four techniques for intermediating China's saving surplus internationally generates claims on foreigners that are in "safe" government hands. That is, they won't be suddenly liquidated if, say, there is suddenly a new scare that the RMB will be appreciated. This minimizes, but does not eliminate, the possibility of hot money inflows back into China that could destabilize the exchange rate and make monetary control more difficult.

Tiny Singapore is also an immature creditor whose own currency is not used for international lending and whose government, like China's, tightly controls overseas financial intermediation. For decades, Singapore's net saving (current account) surpluses have been persistently the world's largest at about 15 to 20 percent of its GNP. To prevent hot money flows, it essentially nationalizes the internal flow of saving by requiring all Singaporeans to deposit what had been as much as 30 percent of their personal incomes in the Singapore Provident Fund—a state-run defined-contribution pension scheme. Then, beyond financing internal investments within Singapore, the proceeds from the Provident Fund are lent to two giant sovereign wealth funds: the Government Overseas Investment Corporation (GIC), which invests in fairly liquid overseas assets, and Temasek, which is more of a risk taker in foreign equities and real estate.

Both the GIC and Temasek are Singapore's answer to minimizing currency risk from international investing. Although the domestic liabilities of the Provident Fund are all in Singapore dollars, their large foreign assets are in various foreign currencies—mainly U.S. dollars. But both agencies are government owned with (implicitly) large capital reserves, so that they can disregard the currency risk. Because the country's large overseas assets are in safe government hands, hot money flows are minimal. The Monetary Authority of Singapore (MAS) controls a gentle "float" of the Singapore dollar against U.S. dollar while holding little in the way of overt official exchange reserves. (The country's unofficial international reserves are the huge assets held by the GIC and Temasek.) The stable exchange rate then anchors Singapore's national price level.

This "Singapore Solution" to international financial intermediation by an immature creditor country, while preserving monetary control, was described in McKinnon (2005, ch. 8). Singapore is too small for Americans and Europeans to complain about its disproportionately large trade (saving) surplus, and demand that the Singapore dollar be appreciated. China (and Japan before it) are not so lucky. Although China's trade surpluses are proportionately much smaller than Singapore's, their large absolute size draws the ire of American mercantilists in the form of "China bashing" for the RMB to be appreciated. Although the common theory that exchange rate appreciation will reduce a saving surplus of a creditor country is wrong (Qiao 2007, McKinnon 2010b), fear of appreciation still induces large hot money inflows into China despite the immunization of its overseas investments—as described by points 1 to 4 above.

Surplus-saving Japan is still an immature international creditor because the yen is not much used to denominate claims on
foreigners. But, unlike China's or Singapore's, Japan's government
does not dominate the international intermediation of its saving
surplus as much. How then is Japan's saving (current account)
surplus financed internationally?

Large Japanese corporations make heavy overseas direct
investments in autos, steel, electronics, and so on. But, in
addition, Japanese banks, insurance companies, and pension
funds have become big holders of liquid assets, at different terms
to maturity, denominated in many foreign currencies such as
Australian, New Zealand, and U.S. dollars—which until fairly
recently had much higher yields than yen assets.

This part of the Japanese system for overseas investment is vulnerable to hot money flows. Over the last 20 years, carry trades out
of low-yield yen assets have been commonplace with a weakening
yen. But they can suddenly reverse, as in 2008 and again in 2012.
The Japanese economy is then vulnerable to sudden runs from
dollars (largely owned by private Japanese financial institutions)
into yen that create damaging sharp appreciations in the "floating"
yen/dollar exchange rate. Investment within Japan is inhibited,
while it becomes more difficult for the stagnant economy to escape
from its zero-interest liquidity trap (McKinnon 2007a).

Through the four measures described above, China has
mitigated—although not escaped from—the immature creditor
dilemma. If it tried to float the RMB, so that the PBC was neither
a buyer nor a seller of foreign exchange, then nonstate Chinese
banks would not accept the risk of financing the huge trade
(saving) surplus by accumulating dollar claims. There would be
no net buyers of the dollars thrown off by China's large export
surplus. The RMB would spiral upward indefinitely against the
dollar with no well-defined upper bound until the PBC was
dragged back in to reset the rate. Despite what Secretary Geithner
suggests, there is no market solution for the exchange rate of a
large immature creditor country.

NOTES

1.   "Flexibility" is a very pleasant word in the English language if only because its opposite connotes pejorative terms such as "rigid," "unbending," "uncaring," and so on. But we should not be deceived by these semantics.
2.   With apologies to the memory of Keynes himself, who, if alive today, might not be a Keynesian.

CHAPTER 12

༄

China and Its Dollar Exchange Rate

A Worldwide Stabilizing Influence?

WITH GUNTHER SCHNABL

China is criticized for keeping its dollar exchange rate fairly stable when it has a large trade (saving) surplus. This criticism is misplaced in two ways. First, no predictable link exists between the exchange rate and the trade balance of an international creditor economy. Second, since 1995, the stable yuan/dollar rate has anchored China's price level and facilitated countercyclical fiscal policies that have smoothed its high real GDP growth. With its now greater GDP, China displaces Japan as the largest economy in East Asia—but with a much stronger stabilizing influence on East Asian neighbors because of its higher economic growth and more stable dollar exchange rate. Now, an ever larger China is an essential stabilizer for the world economy—as exemplified by its prompt and effective fiscal response to the global credit crunch of 2008–09. However, cumulating financial distortions—in China and the United States— threaten to undermine China's growth and its stabilizing influence on the rest of the world.

Since 1994, when China unified its currency, achieving full current-account convertibility by 1996, a stable yuan/dollar rate has anchored China's price level. It has also smoothed real economic growth at an amazingly high annual rate of 9 to 11 percent—almost without precedent in the annals of economic development. Although growth was led by a surge in exports of manufactures in the 1990s, imports also surged, so that China's overall trade remained roughly balanced (table 12.1)—and trade frictions were minimal.

Beginning in 2002, however, China's domestic saving began increasing relative to domestic investment—while national saving in the United States slumped. The result of this international saving imbalance over the next decade was large, growing Chinese bilateral trade surpluses in manufactures with the United States and multilateral surpluses more generally (table 12.1). The corresponding U.S. trade deficits accelerated American industrial decline with politically painful losses of jobs in manufacturing (ch. 6). Fortunately, China had become a full-fledged member of the World Trade Organization (WTO) in 2001. Thus the WTO's rules of the game inhibited outright protectionism by the United States, European Union, Japan, and smaller industrial economies—although antidumping suits against Chinese goods (within the WTO's rubric) remain significant.

Stymied by the WTO but needing an easy political response to the decline in their manufacturing sectors, politicians in the industrial economies led by the United States began to claim that China's heretofore stable exchange rate of 8.28 yuan per dollar was unfairly undervalued and a prime "cause" of China's emerging trade surpluses. Instead, the correct American economic response should have been to increase U.S. tax revenues while curbing both personal and government consumption so as to improve the national investment-saving balance and reduce America's trade deficit. But this proved, and still proves, to be politically too difficult. Far easier to look for a foreign villain—and the yuan/dollar rate was (and is) a politically convenient scapegoat.

Table 12.1.   CHINA'S MULTILATERAL TRADE BALANCE AND BILATERAL
TRADE BALANCE VERSUS THE UNITED STATES

Year	Trade balance (billion US$)	Trade balance (% of GDP)	Bilateral trade balance (billion US$)	Bilateral trade balance (% of GDP)
1980	−1.0	−0.33	−2.8	−0.93
1981	1.0	0.34	−3.2	−1.08
1982	4.8	1.63	−2.5	−0.86
1983	2.6	0.82	−1.0	−0.33
1984	0.1	0.01	−1.5	−0.48
1985	−12.5	−4.04	−2.8	−0.93
1986	−7.4	−2.43	−2.1	−0.69
1987	0.3	0.09	−1.8	−0.55
1988	−4.1	−.98	−3.2	−0.78
1989	−4.9	−1.07	−3.5	−0.75
1990	10.7	2.64	−1.3	−0.32
1991	11.6	2.74	−1.8	−0.43
1992	5.1	1.00	−0.3	−0.06
1993	−11.8	−1.84	6.4	0.99
1994	7.4	1.26	7.4	1.28
1995	12.0	1.58	8.6	1.14
1996	17.6	1.97	10.5	1.18
1997	42.8	4.35	16.5	1.67
1998	43.8	4.19	21.0	2.01
1999	30.6	2.78	22.5	2.05
2000	28.8	2.42	29.8	2.50
2001	28.1	2.13	28.2	2.14
2002	37.4	2.57	42.8	2.94
2003	36.1	2.19	58.7	3.56
2004	49.3	2.54	80.4	4.14
2005	124.7	5.46	114.3	5.01
2006	208.9	7.49	144.6	5.19
2007	307.3	8.80	163.2	4.67
2008	348.7	7.69	171.1	3.77
2009	220.1	4.36	143.6	2.84
2010	183.1	3.11	181.2	3.08
2011	155.1	2.07	202.3	2.70

Source: Datastream.

However, in today's world of globalized finance for trade and investment, the claim that China could reduce its trade (net saving) by appreciating the RMB surplus is specious (chs. 7 and 8; and McKinnon and Schnabl 2009). If the RMB was sharply appreciated, turning China into a higher-cost country in which to invest, globally oriented firms would decamp and invest elsewhere, so that investment in China itself would slump. China's saving-investment balance $(S - I)$ and trade surplus could well increase (chs. 7 and 8)!

The now false idea that the exchange rate can be used to control the trade balance has deep historical roots. In the immediate post–World War II era, when capital controls proliferated outside of the United States and foreign trade was more of a fringe activity, the Western industrial economies were more insular. For that era, using the exchange rate to control a country's trade balance was more plausible—and was central in the influential work of Nobel laureate James Meade, *The Balance of Payments* (1951).

However, by the new millennium, with much greater globalization of trade and finance, Meade's view of the exchange rate had become obsolete—except in economics textbooks. But it is still the intellectual influence behind today's continuing American and European political pressure on China to appreciate the RMB as if that would reduce China's trade surplus. As J. M. Keynes (1935, 383) so aptly put it, "the ideas of economists and political philosophers, both when they are right and when they are wrong, are more powerful than is commonly understood. Indeed, the world is ruled by little else. Practical men, who believe themselves to be exempt from any intellectual influence, are usually the slaves of some defunct economist."

Showing how and why the conventional view linking exchange rate changes to the trade balance breaks down as an economy becomes more open in trade and finance is all well and good. However, we also need an alternative, more positive theory of why a stable dollar exchange rate is the best policy for a rapidly growing emerging market such as China—particularly one with a large saving surplus but whose own private capital market is still too immature to finance it internationally (ch. 11).

THREE STAGES OF THE CHINESE DOLLAR PEG AS A STABILIZER

Why focus just on China's *dollar* exchange rate? Despite monetary turmoil—past and present—emanating from the United States, the world is still mainly on a dollar standard. In East Asia, virtually all imports and exports—including the burgeoning intra-industry trade within the region—are invoiced in dollars. The dollar remains the dominant means of settling international payments among banks, and is the principal intervention currency used by governments, such as China's, for smoothing exchange rate fluctuations. When China stabilizes the yuan/dollar rate, it is really stabilizing the rate against a much broader basket of currencies underlying interregional trade in Asia—and against dollar-based financial markets beyond Asia.

Stage 1. The Dollar Exchange Rate as the Nominal Anchor for the Chinese Economy

Thus in 1994 when China's system of multiple exchange rates was unified and currency restrictions on importing and exporting were eliminated, the yuan/dollar peg became the centerpiece for reducing China previously high and volatile inflation.

In the 1980s, under Deng Xiaoping, China began to move strongly, but gradually, away from a Soviet-style planned economy. Wage and price controls were slowly relaxed. But out of necessity the currency remained inconvertible, with no free arbitrage between domestic prices and the very different relative dollar prices prevailing in international markets. During this 1980–93 period of currency inconvertibility, the "official" yuan/dollar rate was frequently and arbitrarily changed (figure 12.1), and could not have been an anchor for the domestic price level. No open domestic capital market existed for the People's Bank of China (PBC) to execute conventional monetary policy. Monetary control depended on very imperfect credit ceilings on individual banks. The result was high and variable inflation, which peaked out in 1994 at over 20 percent per year (figure 10.4).

But to maintain the new dollar exchange anchor for tradable goods as of 1995, the PBC was "forced" to disinflate sufficiently to maintain 8.28 yuan per dollar over the next decade. By 1997, inflation in China's CPI had fallen to the American level—about 2 percent per year.

From time to time, other countries have used a fixed exchange rate as a "nominal anchor" to kill inflation. What seems virtually unique about the Chinese experience, however, is that inflation remained in abeyance (at least until the worldwide inflation of 2010–11) *and* real GDP growth stabilized at a high level. Figure 10.4 also shows the roller-coaster ride in real growth rates before 1996 during the period of currency inconvertibility, and the subsequent

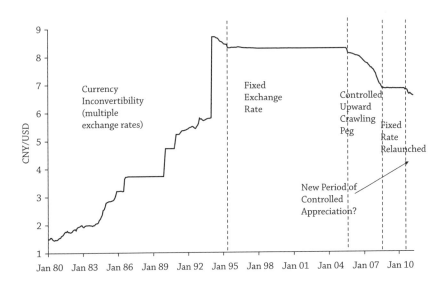

Figure 12.1.
The Yuan-Dollar Exchange Rate, 1980–2011
Source: IMF

much smoother growth in real GNP of around 10 percent per year when the current account had been liberalized under a fixed dollar exchange rate. True, GDP growth slowed to just 8 percent or so in the global crisis of 2008–09, when Chinese exports fell sharply. But in 2010, growth bounced back to its "norm" of about 10 percent.

Stage 2. China as Anchor for the Greater East Asian Economy

China's own monetary and financial stability helped by a stable yuan/dollar rate is important of itself, but it is not the only issue. China has now displaced Japan as the dominant economy in East Asia, both in trade and in size (figure 12.2). Much more rapid growth in GDP for almost a decade and a half, and growing intra-industry trade links, make it not only the engine of high East Asian economic growth but also an anchor for stabilizing that growth.

Japan was dominant in economic size and in East Asian trade flows before 2002 (figure 12.2). Japanese economists linked East Asian development to the so-called flying geese pattern—with Japan as the leading goose. But the Japanese economy never recovered from the collapsed bubbles in its stock and real estate markets in 1990, and remains mired with slow growth and near-zero interest rates today.

More disturbingly for East Asia, the yen/dollar rate fluctuated from 360 per dollar in 1971 to 80 to the dollar in April 1995, and continues to fluctuate widely—albeit closer to 80 than to 360—as shown in figure 12.3. Because the other East Asian economies were "normally" pegged to the dollar, these large fluctuations in the yen/dollar rate created cyclical instability in the smaller East Asian economies (Kwan 2001, McKinnon and Schnabl 2003). When the yen rose against the dollar, direct investment (largely by Japanese firms) flowed out of Japan to Thailand, Korea, and so on, and their exports to Japan boomed. When the yen was weak and Japan

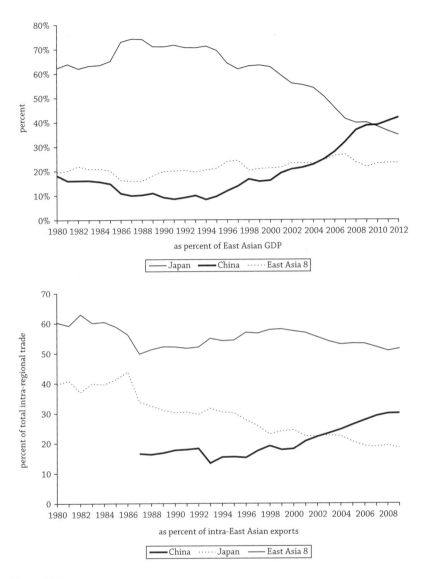

Figure 12.2.
Economic Weights in East Asia
Source: IMF

became more competitive as in the East Asian crisis of 1997–98 (ch. 7), Japanese investment at home boomed, while FDI in other countries in Asia, as well their as exports to Japan, slumped.

So cyclical instability (which China largely avoided) in the smaller East Asian economies was aggravated by fluctuations

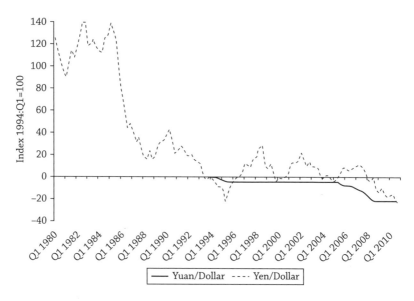

Figure 12.3.
Yen and Yuan against the Dollar
Source: Datastream

in the yen/dollar rate. Before the turn of the millennium, the fluctuations of the yen against the dollar were an important determinant of the business cycle of the smaller East Asian economies. Yen appreciation boosted growth in the smaller East Asian economies, while yen depreciation put a drag on growth. After the turn of the millennium China gained a larger economic weight in East Asia, and the role of the yen/dollar exchange rate for East Asian business cycle fluctuations seems to have faded.

Now in the new millennium and beyond, China has displaced Japan as the dominant East Asian economy—but with the yuan/dollar rate kept much more stable since 1994 than was (and is) the yen/dollar rate (figure 12.2). Thus China is not only the engine of high economic growth for its smaller Asian suppliers and customers, but is also a better anchor for reducing cyclical instability in East Asia. The relatively stable yuan/dollar rate means that an "inadvertent" business cycle is not imparted to the smaller Asian countries (also dollar peggers) in the mode of their earlier experience with Japan and fluctuations in the yen/dollar rate.

Although the yuan/dollar rate has remained relatively stable, on occasion political pressure from the United States has induced periods of gradual RMB appreciation, as from July 2005 to July 2008 (about 6 percent per year), and after June 2010 (figure 12.4). In these intervals, a few other East Asian counties have followed with (small) gradual appreciations. But insofar as these governments intervene, it is still a dollar-based system. (The RMB is not used as an intervention currency because China's financial markets are underdeveloped, with controls on capital inflows.) The dollar remains predominant in interbank markets and as an invoice currency in goods markets. However, the RMB now supplements the dollar's role as an exchange rate anchor in East Asia.

There is a second sense in which China provides stability to East Asia. Major macroeconomic shocks to the East Asian region not originating in China are smoothed by China's stabilizing presence.

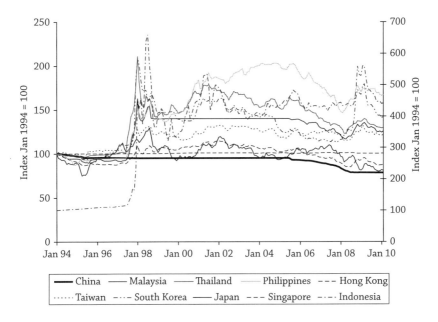

Figure 12.4.
East Asian Exchange Rates against the Dollar
Source: IMF

The upper panel of figure 12.5 shows the real growth patterns in the 10 most important East Asian economies. In the great Asian crisis of 1997–98, one can see the sharp fall to negative growth in most of them—particularly the five in crisis: Indonesia, Korea, Malaysia, Philippines, and Thailand. Meanwhile, during the Asian crisis, China's high growth barely dipped at all—just to 8 percent. Most importantly, despite misplaced foreign advice to depreciate the RMB in the face depreciations by the other nine Asian counties, China opted to keep the yuan/dollar stable at 8.28 during the crisis (figure 12.4). This stable Chinese anchor permitted the other nine East Asian counties to export their way out of the Asian crisis, and thus recover much sooner.

Stage 3. China as a Fiscal Stabilizer on the World Stage

The same pattern of a stabilizing Chinese anchor for the East Asian economies prevails in response to "worldwide" macro shocks, that is, those originating in the center country of the world dollar standard—the United States. The upper panel of figure 12.5 shows the effect of the collapse in 2001–02 in the American stock-market dot-com bubble, when growth slowed sharply in the other nine East Asian economies, but not in China, with its stable yuan/dollar exchange rate. Similarly, in the global credit crunch of 2008–09, growth became negative or slowed sharply in the other East Asian countries but only dipped moderately by one or two percentage points from its very high level in China.

In each of the two major macroeconomic crises, the stable yuan/dollar exchange rate facilitated countercyclical fiscal policy by China. In March 1998, the middle of the Asian crisis, Premier Zhu Rongji announced a major "fiscal" expansion of over one-half trillion U.S. dollars over the next three years. Similarly, in last half of 2008, in the midst of the global credit crunch from failing U.S. and European banks, an ever-larger China began an

Figure 12.5.
Regional and Global Growth Performance
Source: IMF

even bigger multi-trillion-dollar fiscal expansion lasting through 2010. In both cases, increased central and local government spending was financed mainly by enormously increased credits from China's huge state-owned banks. However, by 2011, the Chinese central government began trying to rein in spending by local governments. China had reset its exchange rate at 6.83 yuan per dollar from July 2008 to June 2010 (figure 12.1). So in both cases, the fixed yuan/dollar rate increased the effectiveness of China's countercyclical fiscal expansion—as the old Mundell-Fleming model would have it (Mundell 1963). East Asia and the world economy more generally were indirect beneficiaries.

Can China now be considered a major stabilizing influence worldwide? A glance at the lower panel of figure 12.5 suggests that this is plausible and has already happened. Growth in the European Union, Japan, and the United States plunged well into negative territory in the credit crunch of 2008–09, whereas China's growth only dipped to a comfortable 8 percent per year, and has subsequently recovered to its norm of 10 percent or so. But China itself was sharply impacted by the global credit crunch. To offset the sharp 50 percent fall in its exports in 2008–09, China's massive "fiscal" stimulus, based on the expansion of bank credit in 2008–10, increased demand for both domestic and foreign goods. Imports were sucked in so that China's trade surplus vanished—albeit very briefly—and the other East Asian countries quickly exported their way out of the downturn, helped by a stable yuan/dollar rate. Beyond East Asia, the rest of the world's exports to China also increased in 2009–11.

Although not yet portrayed in any of the figures, it seems that the sovereign debt–cum–banking crisis in Europe beginning in mid-2011 slowed European GDP growth significantly—but not China's. True, this banking crisis interrupted—probably just temporarily—the flow of hot money from the old low-interest industrial economies to the higher-interest emerging markets, as discussed in chapter 5. But high real growth in the Chinese economy was sustained in the face of the American economy's very sluggish recovery from the 2008–09 credit crunch and Europe's travails in 2011.

In 2012, the euro crisis may be weakening Europe's demand for Chinese exports with some slowing of Chinese growth. The big, as yet unresolved, question is "Can China do it again?" That is, can China in 2012–13 again embark on another big countercyclical expansion based on domestic bank credit to preserve aggregate demand in the face of weakening exports? As before, the central government seems to be leaning on state and local governments to invest more in infrastructure projects. But these lower-level governments have larger debt overhangs from their expansiveness in 2008–09. So only time will tell.

Unlike diamonds, sustained high GDP growth in China as a worldwide stabilizer under the dollar standard need not be forever. Some of these sustainability issues are taken up in chapter 13.

PART IV

International Monetary Reform

CHAPTER 13

༄

Rehabilitating the Dollar Standard and the Role of China

The G-2

As international money since 1945, the dollar has shown remarkable resilience in the face of huge upheavals, from the Nixon shock in 1971 to the subprime mortgage crisis of 2008–09 (ch. 4), and to the Bernanke zero-interest rate shock from December 2008 to the present. Its facilitating role in international financial markets is still entrenched as the world's principal invoice, clearing, and reserve currency (ch. 2). It remains invaluable in international commerce.

Yet after the dollar standard's early success from 1945 to the late 1960s in providing a stable nominal anchor for the rest of the world (ch. 3) when China was not yet a major player, its subsequent performance in that role has been lamentable. Because nations have been unable to agree on an alternative international money, I claim that the only feasible international monetary reform is one of rehabilitating the dollar standard.[1] In this concluding chapter, idealized rules of the game—only some of which are new—are proposed to restore a well-functioning world dollar standard.

In the new millennium, China has emerged as the world's largest trading nation and the biggest creditor of the United States.

So it is important to spell out how a modus vivendi between the United States and China—a veritable Group of Two or simply G-2—can operate to rehabilitate the dollar standard. Indeed, without China's (implicit) support, a worldwide monetary crisis from American fiscal profligacy coupled with a credit crunch in the United States will be difficult to avoid.

IDEAL RULES OF THE GAME FOR THE DOLLAR STANDARD

Suppose hypothetically that the U.S. government finally recognizes the central position of the dollar in the world's monetary system and resolves to behave more appropriately as the keeper of the world's money. It embarks on a more outward-looking monetary policy to reduce exchange rate volatility and keep short-term interest rates set comfortably above zero to limit carry trades (chs. 4 and 5). It officially recognizes that America's international borrowing constraint has been unnaturally softened by the special role of the dollar in international finance. Rather than turning protectionist, the U.S. government recognizes that the unduly large trade deficits it has been able finance for decades with impunity by selling Treasury bonds in exchange for foreign manufactured goods has resulted in deindustrialization in the United States (ch. 6).

Even more hopefully, suppose further that the U.S. government comes to understand that these trade deficits cannot be ended, or even alleviated, by devaluing the dollar (chs. 7 and 8), so it stops "bashing" neighboring countries on exchange rate issues. Instead, the United States develops the political will to raise America's net saving rate by ending fiscal deficits and encouraging more saving in the private sector. As the trade deficit with its transfer of foreign manufactures to the United States naturally declines, the dollar's effective exchange rate need not, and best not, change (ch. 9). But the American manufacturing sector would begin to recover.

With a rehabilitated dollar standard, foreign governments would become resigned to the inevitable asymmetry between center and periphery in current financial arrangements based on the dollar. As debtors or creditors, they would move to minimize volatility arising out of currency mismatches (ch. 11). In crisis situations, the IMF would remain the lender of first resort and stay as crisis manager. But the United States itself would still be the lender of last resort. With the possible exception of an implosion in the euro zone, the combined IMF–United States entity would have sufficient dollar resources to limit financial crises around the world.

To show how our present international monetary order should be modified, 10 idealized rules for the dollar standard of the future are set out in box 13.1. Reflecting the inherent asymmetry in the world's money machine, the first six rules apply to the United States, and the second four rules apply to emerging markets on the periphery with immature capital markets—including large rapidly growing countries such as China and Brazil.

These 10 idealized rules are hardly all-encompassing.[2] The European bloc, with the euro as the central currency, really does not fit comfortably into this analytical framework. Moreover, as of the current writing, the European Monetary Union is in turmoil—for which a meaningful set of rules would be beyond the scope of this book. Small countries independent of any bloc would be free to choose what monetary-cum-exchange-rate system they wanted. Yet for larger countries, these rules show how a better-functioning dollar standard could greatly reduce recurring currency crises in the world at large and financial volatility in the United States itself.

In light of the analysis contained in earlier chapters of this book, each of the 10 rules in box 13.1 is virtually self-explanatory. If the dollar standard is truly rehabilitated, U.S. short-term monetary policy would be more oriented toward multilateral exchange stability, and fiscal policy oriented toward eliminating the country's

---

Box 13.1

NEW RULES OF THE GAME FOR AN
IDEALIZED DOLLAR STANDARD

UNITED STATES

Rule 1. In the long run, limit inflation and stabilize the domestic and foreign purchasing power of the dollar so as to provide a nominal anchor for the price levels of other countries.

Rule 2. In the short run, raise interest rates to prevent outflows of "hot" money to other countries collectively when the dollar is weak, and vice versa. Keep interest rates comfortably above zero.

Rule 3. In noncrisis periods, remain passive in the foreign exchanges: allow foreigners to transact freely in dollars and set their dollar exchange rates without being "bashed." No capital controls for the center country.

Rule 4. The IMF acts as lender of first resort to individual countries in crisis. The United States acts as lender of last resort through dollar swaps and similar devices to overcome dollar liquidity crises more generally.

Rule 5. Do not force developing countries to open their financial markets internationally or to abandon capital controls. Cease pushing entry of American banks and other financial institutions into their domestic economies.

Rule 6. Limit or reverse current account deficits by increasing domestic saving, government and private.

EMERGING MARKETS

Rule 7. Retain current-account currency convertibility under the IMF's Article VIII, but recognize the problem of currency mismatches. Restrain foreign exchange exposure by banks and other financial institutions, if necessary by capital controls.

7A: Debtor economies: Limit buildup of short-term liquid dollar liabilities.

7B: Creditor economies: Limit "overhangs" of liquid dollar assets.

Rule 8. Recognize that pegging to the dollar may be necessary to reduce risk in countries with immature domestic financial markets—particularly if they are either large dollar debtors or large dollar creditors.

Rule 9. Aim for mutual exchange rate stability within natural economic regions such as East Asia. Set long-term dollar exchange rate objectives for the group.

Rule 10. Hold official exchange reserves mainly in dollar assets. If necessary, supplement with regional swap agreements—as in East Asia.

huge saving deficiency and accompanying trade deficit. Then U.S. long-term monetary policy could focus on stabilizing America's *domestic* price level—perhaps by adopting a 2 percent annual inflation target for its CPI. With a more stable domestic price level and exchange rates, and with moderately variable interest rates comfortably above zero, the United States would then return to being a stable nominal anchor for the price levels and monetary policies of most other counties—as was largely true of the Bretton Woods system of fixed exchange rates in the 1950s and 1960s (ch. 3).

But this time around, a collective agreement to fix dollar exchange parities (as per the IMF's original Article IV) would be unnecessary, provided that China retains its dollar peg (see below) and countries continue to adhere to Article VIII— the commitment to current-account convertibility. With a stable nominal anchor, most countries would voluntarily return to dollar pegging[3]—or at least to tracking the dollar so as to avoid large changes in their dollar-cum-yuan exchange rates. And the United States would benignly neglect such machinations without "bashing" any country on its exchange rate policies.

In this brave new world, the dollar would retain its current role as the facilitator of multilateral exchange among nations (ch. 2). But now this facilitating role would be enhanced as exchange rate fluctuations moderated—as per rules 2, 8, and 9—so as to reduce banking, that is, money-changing, risks. For emerging markets and developing countries more generally, dollar dominance would still lead to currency mismatches in those that were either debtors or creditors (rule 7) as it now does. But again, greater exchange stability would mitigate the risks involved.

EMERGING CHINA AS A PILLAR OF THE DOLLAR STANDARD

Beyond box 13.1, China is not just another "emerging market." Measured by the sum of its exports and imports, it is now the world's largest trading economy—and has eclipsed Japan as the center of the trading system in Asia (ch. 12). Nobody can predict the future. But by extrapolating possible trends, figure 13.1 projects that, around 2021, China's *nominal* GDP will approach that of the United States even without further renminbi appreciation.[4] If there is substantial appreciation of the RMB (a decidedly bad idea; see chapters 5 and 12), then the approach would be quicker. Of course, with its immense population, China's "real" per capita GDP will still remain much less than America's for several decades.

China has also become very large financially. Figure 13.2 shows that, in 2011, its official exchange reserves of over \$3.2 trillion now dwarf Japan's second-highest holding of \$1.2 trillion. Countries don't reveal the currency composition of their reserves, but before the euro crisis of 2011–12, the IMF estimated that about 65 percent of official reserves were in dollar-denominated

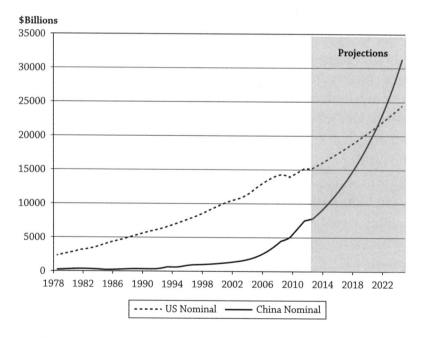

Figure 13.1.
US and China Nominal GDP History and Projection
Source: International Financial Statistics, IMF, author's projection

instruments. China's huge buildup of official exchange reserves reflects both the cumulative effect of its large trade surpluses over many years, not offset by capital outflows, and, increasingly, "hot" money inflows. The U.S. Fed's unfortunate policy of near-zero interest rates and threats of RMB appreciation from American China "bashing" are the main source of China's hot money inflow (ch. 5).

Surprisingly, despite some political and economic frictions with the United States, China has—more or less inadvertently—become a pillar of the dollar standard. Consider just three aspects of this supporting role:

1. *The "snowball" effect* (Krugman 1984): The great expansion of Chinese trade with other emerging markets and countries producing primary products throughout the world, where the dollar is both the invoice currency for goods and the clearing currency for making international payments (ch. 2),

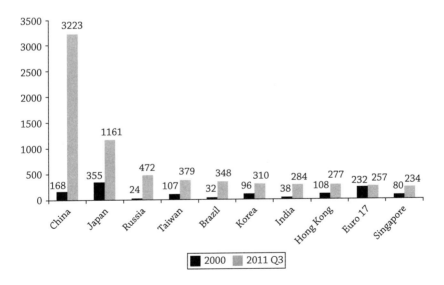

Figure 13.2.
Major Foreign Reserve Holders, Oil Exporters Excluded (2000 vs. 2011 Q3, in Billions of USD)
Source: International Financial Statistics, IMF

reduces transaction costs and increases the liquidity of dollar-based markets. Figure 13.3 shows the relative increase in China's imports (mainly of primary products) from Asia, Africa, and Latin America—coupled with a relative decline in imports from the more mature industrial economies of the United States, the European Union, and Japan. But these shifts are only relative: China's trade everywhere is growing fast in absolute terms.

2. *The macro stabilization effect*: Since 1994, China has succeeded in following a countercyclical fiscal (credit) policy so as to stabilize its own GDP growth at a high level, which somewhat buffers cyclical instability emanating from the United States (ch. 12).

3. *The finance effect*: China provides finance for large American fiscal deficits. If, following China, foreigners collectively

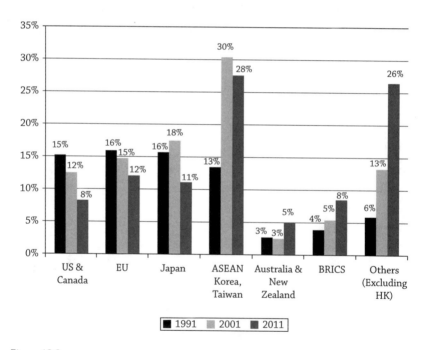

Figure 13.3.
China's Trade Partners: Imports from China (percentage based on total imports)
Source: China Customs Statistics
BRICS: Brazil, Russia, India, South Africa. EU in 1991 refer to EEC, EFTA (less Switzerland), Bulgaria, Hungary, Malta, Poland, Romania, Czechoslovakia

ceased buying Treasury bonds and other dollar assets, a
credit crunch in the United States would ensue (figure 13.4
and chapter 6).

These three effects are hardly recognized in the economic literature, let alone in political discussion between governments.
Yet they go well beyond the conventional wisdom on comparative advantage, where the U.S. consumer greatly benefits
from a plethora of Chinese-made consumption goods—while
China has greatly benefited from access to U.S. technology
and capital goods. Although this conventional view is all well
and good the three effects cited above show that the mutual
gains to the Sino-American economic interaction are much
greater than this received wisdom would suggest.

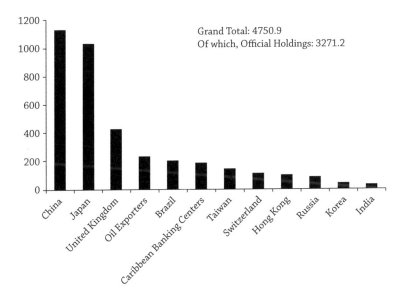

Figure 13.4.
U.S. Treasury Securities Holdings by Selected Foreign Countries (November 2011, in
billions of dollars)
Source: U.S. Department of the Treasury

THE SAVING (TRADE) IMBALANCE

However, the current economic sticking point in the political relationship between the Chinese and American governments is the trade imbalance. Table 12.1 in chapter 12 shows that this imbalance between the two countries became substantial after 2000, continuing to the present day. Indeed, China's bilateral trade surplus with the United States is now greater than its overall trade surplus; see figure 13.5 and table 12.1. This suggests that, in determining the U.S. trade deficit in 2012, the pull from the American saving deficiency is now stronger than the push from surplus saving in China—although both are important. Otherwise, China's trade surplus would be larger on a multilateral basis, as it was back in 2006–09 (figure 13.5).

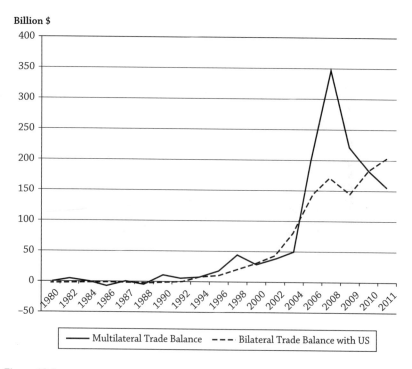

Figure 13.5.
China's Multilateral (Overall) Trade Surplus and Bilateral Trade Surplus versus the United States

Because of myopia on the causes of the U.S. trade deficit, there has been an American political backlash against China. The political representatives of firms and trade unions involved in U.S. manufacturing misdiagnose the problem: they accuse China of deliberately undervaluing the RMB against the dollar, or engaging in covert protectionism by Chinese state-owned enterprises. Instead, to reduce the trade deficit, they should be lobbying the Congress to end the U.S. fiscal deficit (the saving deficiency) by cutting expenditures or raising taxes.

This current story is even more depressing (at least to the author!) because it has happened before. In the 1970s and 1980s, Japan was the up-and-coming manufacturing nation with very high growth in both exports and GDP. But in the 1980s American net saving fell because President Ronald Reagan's huge defense buildup resulted in a large fiscal deficit—whence the famous U.S. twin deficits: fiscal and trade. In the 1980s, Japan began to run large trade (saving) surpluses in manufactures with the United States. The result was "Japan bashing," with the threat of severe American protectionist measures unless Japan allowed the yen to appreciate. Unfortunately, Japan acquiesced to this political pressure, and the yen rose from 360 to the dollar in 1971 to touch 80 to the dollar by April 1995. This huge appreciation then knocked Japan off its high growth path into semistagnation and deflation *without* reducing Japan's trade surplus as a proportion of its GDP (McKinnon and Ohno 1997, Qiao 2007).

Figure 13.6 shows "Japan bashing" back in the 1980s and early 1990s that was provoked by Japan's having a high bilateral trade surplus with the United States. This is then succeeded by "China bashing" after 2000 as China's bilateral surplus with the United States grows bigger than the declining Japanese bilateral surplus. U.S. policymaking in both periods was (is) under the sway of the Exchange Rate and Trade Balance Fallacy (ch. 1). American politicians and many economists still believe (mistakenly) that if China accelerated the appreciation of the RMB against the dollar, the trade imbalance between the two countries would diminish.

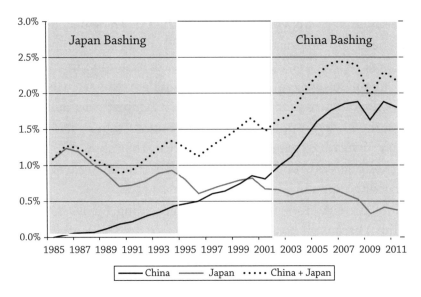

Figure 13.6.
Bilateral Trade Balances of Japan and China versus the United States (percentage of U.S. GDP, 1985–2011)
Source: U.S. Census Bureau

However, in today's world, this saving imbalance between China and the United States is not one-sided. True, the American fiscal deficits of the G. W. Bush and Obama administrations greatly reduce(d) government saving; and the huge U.S. housing bubble from 2003 to 2008 created a false wealth effect that reduced private saving as well. But China has had the inverse problem of "surplus" saving. It has resulted both in excess low-quality investment by local governments and state-owned enterprises (ch. 12) and in an unnaturally high bilateral trade surplus with the United States. They are not unrelated. The very low interest policy of Fed chairman Bernanke has aggravated both problems.

THE LOW INTEREST RATE CONUNDRUM

On the American side, in early 2012 the Fed officially forecast that it would keep short-term interest rates close to zero through

2014. Since longer-term interest rates simply reflect short rates expected in the future plus a liquidity premium, 10-year rates on U.S. Treasuries have been driven down to just 1.65 percent in 2012—and seem set to stay there. Because long rates no longer rise from fear of future fiscal deficits generating a credit crunch, Congress and the president no longer face market discipline when they overspend or undertax. What used to be called the "Bond Market Vigilantes" are missing (McKinnon 2011b).[5] The unchecked U.S. fiscal deficit does not lead to higher interest rates and a credit crunch because the U.S. trade deficit widens and induces the People's Bank of China, and central banks from other emerging markets facing upward pressure on their exchange rates, to buy dollars—many of which are then switched into U.S. Treasury bonds.

Chapter 5 also showed that the Fed's policy of near-zero short-term interest rates, in force since December 2008, disrupts internal financial intermediation. Lending within the U.S. wholesale interbank market is constricted, which increases the risks seen by "retail" bank lenders to firms and households. The disappointingly slow recovery of the U.S. GDP after the 2008–09 downturn (figures 13.7a and 13.7b) is often ascribed to the slow, or nonexistent, growth in normal short-term bank credit—unlike most recoveries from cyclical downturns. Moreover, near zero interest rates is forcing the closure of money market mutual funds (MMMF) for fear of "breaking the buck," as described in chapter 5. And as short-term financial intermediaries, these MMMF had become almost as large as banks themselves.

In the medium term, defined-benefit pension funds, either public such as those run by state and local governments or private such as those run by insurance companies, cannot now earn enough on their assets to cover their contracted future pension payouts. And these insurance-type financial intermediaries have been the main source of long-term finance within the American economy. So the Fed's protracted policy of near-zero interest

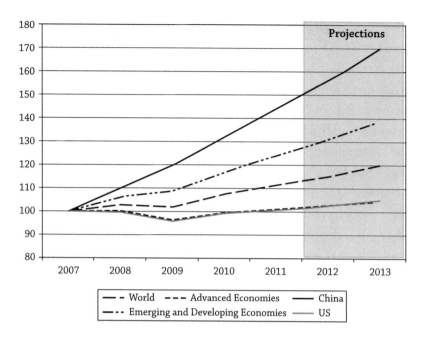

Figure 13.7a.
World's Real GDP in Recoveries (2007 = 100)

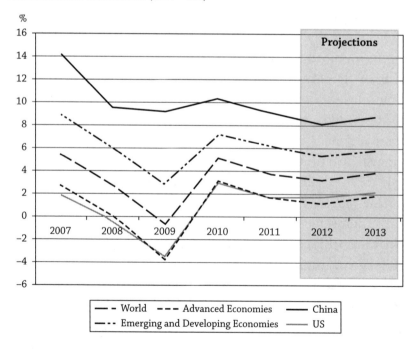

Figure 13.7b.
Real GDP Growth Rate in Recoveries
Source: Martin Wolf, *Financial Times*, February 8, 2012

rates has the making of a financial disaster within the United States itself.

On the Chinese side, the U.S. Federal Reserve's ultralow interest rates at the center of the world dollar standard result in a form of *financial repression* (Lardy 2008; ch. 12). The PBC is forced to keep Chinese bank deposit and loan interest rates far below the natural rate of interest associated with a high-growth economy (table 13.1). Even so, hot money flows in through somewhat porous capital controls, and the PBC is forced to buy U.S. dollars to keep the exchange rate stable. (The inflow of hot money is accentuated by expected appreciation of the RMB.) Some of this excess money creation is sterilized, but potential inflationary pressure in China's CPI remains. How does the resulting financial repression distort China's economy?

1. Households see a deposit interest rate below the rate of inflation—a form of taxation that reduces household income and consumption (figure 13.8).

Table 13.1. INTEREST RATES AND GDP GROWTH FOR U.S. AND CHINA

	China				**United States**			
	Deposit rate	Lending rate	Interbank overnight rate	GDP growth	Deposit rate	Lending rate	Federal funds rate	GDP growth
2000	2.25	5.85		8.37	6.65	9.23	6.24	6.39
2001	2.25	5.58		10.41	3.73	6.92	3.89	3.36
2002	1.98	5.31	2.4	10.50	1.88	4.67	1.67	3.46
2003	1.98	5.31	2.18	13.41	1.23	4.12	1.13	4.70
2004	2.25	5.58	2.01	17.69	1.79	4.34	1.35	6.51
2005	2.25	5.58	2.01	16.38	3.76	6.19	3.21	6.49
2006	2.52	6.12	1.31	18.76	5.27	7.96	4.96	6.02
2007	4.14	7.47	1.97	19.62	5.25	8.05	5.02	4.95
2008	2.25	5.31	2.21	18.46	3.05	5.09	1.93	2.19
2009	2.25	5.31	.83	9.57	1.12	3.25	0.16	-1.74
2010	2.5	5.56	2.24	12.88	0.518	3.25	0.17	3.57

Source: Datastream; GDP for 2010 are IMF staff estimates; values for Chinese deposit and lending rates are from November 2010.

2. Some enterprises receive a substantial subsidy in the form of cheap credit (the standard bank loan rate in 2010 was 5.56 percent), creating great excess demand. At this centrally mandated low interest rate, the state-owned banks pick just the safest borrowers—which are large state-owned enterprises.

3. With the credit subsidy, the profitability of large state-owned enterprises (SOEs) has surged in recent years—and there is no policy of remitting these profits to households, whence the proclivity of SOEs to invest in fixed assets. Investment has grown to a remarkable 45 percent of GDP (figure 13.8). At near-zero real rates of interest, the quality of many of

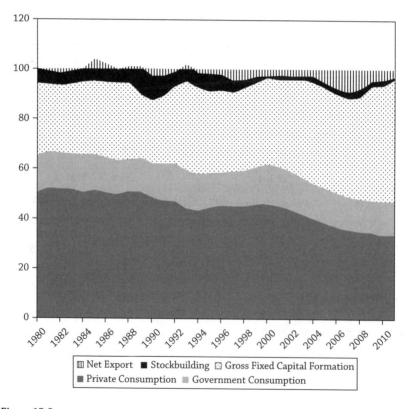

Figure 13.8.
China GDP Composition, 1980–2011
Source: Economist Intelligence Unit (EIU). Estimation value for 2011

these investments cannot be high. Moreover, the shares of personal income and private consumption are falling (figure 13.8). In 2012, China's private consumption of 35 percent of GDP was only half of the U.S. level.

4. Because formal bank rates of interest have to be kept low, the banks cannot really lend to small and medium-size firms or households—where interest rates would have to be in the range of 10 to 20 percent. So a number of "shadow" banks have come into existence to lend to small firms outside the control of China's regulatory authorities.

5. The real exchange rate, that is, the relative price of nontradables to tradables, has not appreciated enough because of the need to sterilize the hot money inflows (ch. 12). So China remains overly competitive in international trade.

A MODUS VIVENDI BETWEEN CHINA AND THE UNITED STATES?

In the short run, the two countries can live comfortably with each other if the U.S. Federal Reserve Bank gradually raises its federal funds interest rate toward some modest level, say 2 percent—and abandons its policy of talking down long rates by threatening to keep short rates near zero indefinitely. This win-win policy change would benefit both countries: relaxing constraints on bank-based or MMMF financial intermediation in the United States, while curbing inflationary inflows of hot money into China, which keep Chinese interest rates too low.

To correct the trade imbalance in the longer run, the need for substantial, but complementary, structural adjustments in both countries' saving rates cannot be ignored. To comfortably finance its "normal" level of domestic investment of about 17 percent of GDP without relying on net borrowing from foreigners, the United States must restore its domestic saving to about the same level. While U.S. households may be induced to save more, the bulk of the adjustment must be to curb public sector dissaving, that is, to eliminate the large fiscal deficits of the federal government by some combination of cutting expenditures and increasing tax revenues.

To right its distribution of income between households and enterprises, China must arrange for regular dividend payouts from enterprises to households. The household share of disposable income in GDP has fallen too much as enterprise profits have ballooned since the middle of the last decade. Thus the problem is not that the household propensity to save is too high, but rather that enterprises save too much—mostly in the form of excess investment in fixed assets. Rapid wage increases are also part of the answer, and Chinese wages can be expected to grow faster when the yuan/dollar rate is stable (ch. 10).

If both countries proceed in parallel, with American saving increasing as Chinese saving falls, then the trade imbalance can be reduced smoothly without wrenching changes in relative prices or the need for the yuan/dollar rate to change—as shown in chapter 9 (no more China bashing on the exchange rate). Gradually correcting the saving imbalance between the two countries with a stable exchange rate is the key to promoting a "soft" landing (ch. 6) without a credit crunch in the United States, or a wave of protectionism against Chinese exports. Then the modus vivendi between the two countries will be sustainable.

What about other emerging markets and industrial countries like Japan? Under a rehabilitated dollar standard, a stable yuan/dollar rate is also a vital cog in inducing other countries to stabilize their dollar exchange rates—as per rules 7 and 8 in box 13.1 and chapter 9. If the world's largest trading economy stabilized its dollar exchange rate, this would provide an even stronger nominal anchor and incentive for others, such as Japan, to do the same. With the G-2 seen to be cooperating, a new system of stable dollar exchange rates for both industrial countries and emerging markets would emerge without a new formal treaty like that associated with Bretton Woods in 1945.

Alternatively, however, suppose there is no modus vivendi. That is, U.S. interest rates stay close to zero and there is no mutual saving adjustment between the China and the United States as the American fiscal system continues to hemorrhage. This opens up the possibility of a new credit crunch in the United States. Chapter 6 described how the 1991–92 U.S. credit crunch resulted from the sudden interruption of capital inflows from Germany and Japan, which at that time had been covering the U.S. fiscal deficit. Although temporary, the 1991–92 U.S. downturn was sufficiently sharp to block the re-election of George H. Bush in the fall of 1992—a re-election that seemed almost certain after the U.S. victory in the Gulf War of 1991. But banks stopped normal commercial lending and bought Treasury bonds instead.

Today, the size of the U.S. fiscal deficit—and the deficiency in American saving more generally—is now larger. In addition, the stock overhang reflecting net American indebtedness to foreigners is much larger. So the potential for a much sharper and prolonged credit crunch in the United States is there.

Foreigners, particularly central banks, will stop lending to the United States only if a precipitate general loss of confidence in the dollar standard leads them to forgo stabilizing their dollar exchange rates—and instead allow appreciation(s) to occur. If emerging markets all appreciate together, the loss of international competitiveness by any one of them would be minimized. Nobody knows when or what might trigger such a loss in confidence. But leading candidates are (1) the Federal Reserve's near-zero interest rate policy, (2) "China bashing" to force China give up on stabilizing its dollar exchange rate that signals other EMs to do the same, and (3) the U.S. political paralysis over the never-ending fiscal deficit.

Despite the dollar standard's remarkably long hegemony since 1945, the world's one and only money machine is in a fragile state. And any sudden breakdown would be extremely disruptive for all nations, including China and, most of all, the United States itself. But euro related problems aside, constructive cooperation between the G-2 can avoid such a breakdown outside of Europe.

NOTES

1. Increases in Special Drawing Rights (SDRs) by the IMF for its member countries
    have been touted as a partial substitute for the dollar. But since its first issue in
    1972, and greatly expanded issue in 2010, SDRs have had a negligible effect on
    dollar holdings in official exchange reserves. As international money, SDRs are
    essentially flawed because they have no basis in private international commerce
    (McKinnon 1979).
2. Indeed they arise naturally out of the author's previous efforts to describe the
    continually evolving postwar dollar standard by a series of rule boxes (McKinnon
    1993).
3. As they largely did from the mid-1980s to the global credit crisis of 2008–09.
    This informal pegging to the dollar has been christened as "Bretton Woods II" by
    Dooley, Folkerts-Landau, and Garber (2003).
4. Assumption: U.S. real GDP annual growth at 2.5 percent, inflation 1.5 percent;
    China real GDP annual growth at 8 percent, inflation 4 percent, USD/RMB rate
    stays at 2012 level.
5. See my "Where are the Bond Vigilantes?" in the *Wall Street Journal* Sept 30, 2011.

REFERENCES

Barro, Robert J. 2001. "Economic Growth in East Asia before and after the Financial Crisis." NBER Working Paper No. 8330.

Bergsten, Fred. 2010. "Correcting the Chinese Exchange Rate: An Action Plan." Testimony before the Committee on Ways and Means, US House of Representatives. *Congressional Record*, March 24.

Calvo, Guillermo, and Carmen Reinhart. 2000. "Fixing for Your Life." NBER Working Paper No. 8006.

Chinoy, Sajjid Z. 2001. "Currency Risk Premia and Unhedged, Foreign-Currency Borrowing in Emerging Markets." Ph.D. dissertation, Department of Economics, Stanford University.

Cline, William. 2005. *The United States as a Debtor Nation*. Washington, D.C.: Institute for International Economics, Center for Global Development.

Cline, William, and John Williamson. 2009. "Estimates of Fundamental Equilibrium Exchange Rates." Peterson Institute for International Economics, Policy Brief No. 09-10.

De Grauwe, Paul, and Gunther Schnabl. 2005. "Nominal versus Real Convergence with Respect to EMU Accession—EMU Entry Scenarios for the New Member States." *Kyklos* 58:481–99.

Despres, Emile. 1965. "A Proposal for Strengthening the Dollar." Research Center in Economic Growth, Stanford University, Memo No. 38, May.

Despres, Emile, Charles Kindleberger, and Walter Salant. 1966. "The Dollar and World Liquidity: A Minority View." *The Economist* (London), February 5, 526–29.

Dooley, Michael P., David Folkerts-Landau, and Peter Garber. 2003. "An Essay on the Revived Bretton Woods System." NBER Working Paper No. 9971.

Eichengreen, Barry, and Ricardo Hausmann. 1999. "Exchange Rate Regimes and Financial Fragility." NBER Working Paper No. 7418.

———. 2003. "Currency Mismatches, Debt Intolerance and Original Sin: Why They Are Not the Same and Why It Matters." NBER Working Paper No. 10036.

Frenkel, Jacob A., and Michael L. Mussa. 1980. "The Efficiency of the Foreign Exchange Market and Measures of Turbulence." *American Economic Association Papers and Proceedings* 70:374–81.

———. 1985. "Asset Markets, Exchange Rates and the Balance of Payments." In Ronald W. Jones and Peter B. Kenen, eds., *Handbook of International Economics*, vol. 2, 679–747. Amsterdam: North-Holland.

Freitag, Stephan, and Gunther Schnabl. 2010. "Reverse Causality in Global Current Accounts." ECB Working Paper No. 1208.

Friedman, Milton. 1953. "The Case for Flexible Exchange Rates." In *Essays in Positive Economics*. Chicago: University of Chicago Press.

———. 1968. "The Role of Monetary Policy." *American Economic Review* 58:1–17.

Goldstein, Morris. 2004. "China and the Renminbi Exchange Rate." In C. Fred Bergsten and John Williamson, eds., *Dollar Adjustment: How Far? Against What?*, 197–230. Washington, D.C.: Institute for International Economics.

Gourinchas, Pierre-Olivier, and Helene Rey. 2005. "International Financial Adjustment." NBER Working Paper No. 11155, February.

Goyal, Rishi, and Ronald McKinnon. 2001. "Japan's Negative Risk Premium in Interest Rates: The Liquidity Trap and Fall in Bank Lending." *World Economy* 24:279–315.

Green, Stephen. 2011. "China, In, Out, Shake It About." *Global Research*, Standard Chartered, May 5.

Hale, Galina, and Cheryl Long. 2010. "If You Try, You'll Get By: Chinese Private Firms' Efficiency Gains from Overcoming Financial Constraints." Photocopy.

Hamada, Koichi, and Akiyoshi Horiuchi. 1987. "The Political Economy of the Financial Market." In Kozo Yamamura and Yasukichi Yasuba, eds., *The Political Economy of Japan*, vol. 1, *The Domestic Transformation*, 23–262. Stanford, Calif.: Stanford University Press.

Hanke, Steve. 2010. "The Great 18-Year Real Estate Cycle." *Globe Asia*, 22–24.

Hanke, Steve. 2011. "Malfeasant Central Bankers, Again." *GlobeAsia*, November, 20–22.

Hayek, Friedrich von. 1929. *Geldtheorie und Konjunkturtheorie*. Vienna: Hölder-Pichler-Tempsky.

Hoffmann, Andreas, and Gunther Schnabl. 2011. "A Vicious Cycle of Financial Market Exuberance, Panics and Asymmetric Policy Response—an Overinvestment View." *World Economy* 34:382–403.

Horsefield, J. Keith, ed. 1969. *The International Monetary Fund, 1945–1965: Twenty Years of International Monetary Cooperation*. Vol. 3, *Documents*. Washington, D.C.: International Monetary Fund.

Johnson, Harry. 1958. "Towards a General Theory of the Balance of Payments." In *International Trade and Economic Growth: Studies in Pure Theory*. London: Allen and Unwin.

Kenen, Peter. 2002. "The Euro versus the Dollar: Will There Be Struggle for Dominance?" *Journal of Policy Modeling* 24:347–54.

Keynes, John Maynard. 1936. *The General Theory of Employment, Interest, and Money*. London: Macmillan.

Kindleberger, Charles. 1965. "Balance of Payments Deficits and the International Market for Liquidity." *Princeton Essays in International Finance* No. 46, May.

Kraay, Art, and Jaume Ventura. 2000. "Current Accounts in Debtor and Creditor Countries." *Quarterly Journal of Economics* 115:1137–66.

Krugman, Paul. 1984. "The International Role of the Dollar: Theory and Prospect." In John F. O. Bilson and Richard C. Marston, eds., *Exchange Rate Theory and Practice*, 261–78. Chicago: University of Chicago Press.

———. 2010. "Chinese New Year." *New York Times*, January 1.

Kwan, C. H. 2001. *Yen Bloc: Toward Economic Integration in Asia*. Washington, D.C.: Brookings Institution Press.

Jones, Ronald W. 1975. "Presumption and the Transfer Problem." *Journal of International Economics* 5:263–74.

Lardy, Nicholas. 2003. "United States–China Ties: Reassessing the Economic Relationship." Testimony before the House Committee on International Relations. *Congressional Record*, October 21.

———. 2005. "China: The Great New Economic Challenge?" In C. Fred Bergsten, ed., *The United States and the World Economy: Foreign Economic Policy for the Next Decade*, 121–41. Washington, D.C.: Institute for International Economics.

———. 2008. "Financial Repression in China." Peterson Institute for International Economics, Policy Brief No. 08-8, September.

Lindbeck, Assar. 1979. *Inflation and Unemployment in Open Economies*. Amsterdam: North-Holland.

Marston, Richard C. 1985. "Stabilization Policies in Open Economies." In R. W. Jones and Peter Kenen, eds., *Handbook of International Economics*, vol. 2, 859–916. Amsterdam: North-Holland.

McKinnon, Ronald. 1969. "Private and Official International Money: The Case for the Dollar." *Princeton Essays in International Finance* No. 74, April.

———. 1979. *Money in International Exchange: The Convertible Currency System*. New York: Oxford University Press.

———. 1982. "Currency Substitution and Instability in the World Dollar Standard." *American Economic Review* 72:320–33.

———. 1990. "The Exchange Rate and the Trade Balance: Insular versus Open Economies." *Open Economies Review* 1:17–37.

———. 1993. "The Rules of the Game: International Money in Historical Perspective." *Journal of Economic Literature* 21:1–44.

———. 2005. *Exchange Rates under the East Asian Dollar Standard: Living with Conflicted Virtue*. Cambridge: MIT Press. Chinese translation 2005, Japanese 2007.

———. 2005. "Trapped by the Dollar Standard." *Journal of Policy Modeling* 27:477–85.

———. 2007a. "Japan's Deflationary Hangover and the Syndrome of the Ever-Weaker Yen." *Singapore Economic Review* 52:309–34.

———. 2007b. "The Transfer Problem in Reducing the U.S. Current Account Deficit." *Journal of Policy Modeling* 29:669–75.

———. 2007c. "The Worth of the Dollar." SIEPR Policy Brief, Stanford University, February. Reprinted from *Wall Street Journal*, December 16, 2006.

———. 2007d. "Why China Should Keep Its Dollar Peg: A Historical Perspective from Japan." *International Finance* 10:43–70.

———. 2009. "U.S. Exit Strategies and Zero Interest Rates." *Journal of Economic Asymmetries* 6, no. 3: 7–13.

———. 2010a. "Why Exchange Rate Changes Will Not Correct Global Imbalances." SIEPR Policy Brief, Stanford University, August.

———. 2010b. "Why China Shouldn't Float: There Is No Market Exchange Rate Solution for an Immature Creditor Country." *International Economy*, Fall, 34–35.

———. 2011a. "The Return of Stagflation." *Wall Street Journal*, May 24.

———. 2011b. "Where Are the Bond Vigilantes?" *Wall Street Journal*, September 30.

McKinnon, Ronald, and Kenichi Ohno. 1997. *Dollar and Yen: Resolving Economic Conflict between the United States and Japan*. Cambridge: MIT Press. Japanese translation 1998, Chinese 1999.

McKinnon, Ronald, and Huw Pill. 1996. "Credible Liberalizations and International Capital Flows: The Overborrowing Syndrome." In Takatoshi Ito and Anne O.

Krueger, eds., *Financial Deregulation and Integration in East Asia*, 7–42. Chicago: University of Chicago Press.

———. 1999. "Exchange Rate Regimes for Emerging Markets: Moral Hazard and International Overborrowing." *Oxford Review of Economic Policy* 15:19–38.

McKinnon, Ronald, and Gunther Schnabl. 2003. "Synchronized Business Cycles in East Asia and Fluctuations in the Yen/Dollar Exchange Rate." *World Economy* 26:1067–88.

———. 2004a. "The East Asian Dollar Standard, Fear of Floating, and Original Sin." *Review of Development Economics*, August 8, 331–60.

———. 2004b. "A Return to Soft Dollar Pegging in East Asia? Mitigating Conflicted Virtue." *International Finance* 7, no. 2: 169–201.

———. 2006. "China's Exchange Rate and International Adjustment in Wages, Prices, and Interest Rates: Japan Déjà Vu?" *CESifo Studies* 52, no. 2: 276–303.

———. 2009. "The Case for Stabilizing China's Exchange Rate: Setting the Stage for Fiscal Expansion." *China and the World Economy* 17 (January–February): 1–32.

———. 2010a. "A Reply to Krugman." *International Economy*, Winter, 37–39.

———. 2010b. "Why Exchange Rate Changes Will Not Correct Global Imbalances." Policy Brief, Stanford Institute for Policy Research, June.

———. 2011. "China and Its Dollar Exchange Rate: A Worldwide Stabilizing Influence?" CESifo Working Paper No. 3449, May.

Meade, James. 1951. *The Balance of Payments*. New York: Oxford University Press.

Milesi-Ferretti, Gian Maria, and Assaf Razin. 1998. "Current Account Reversals and Currency Crises: Empirical Regularities." IMF Working Paper No. 98/89, June.

Mundell, Robert, 1963. "Capital Mobility and Stabilization Policy under Fixed and Flexible Exchange Rates." *Canadian Journal of Economics and Political Science* 29:479–85.

Noland, Marcus, Li-Gang Liu, Sherman Robinson, and Zhi Wang. 1998. "Global Economic Effects of the Asian Currency Devaluations." Institute for international Economics, Washington, D.C.

Obstfeld, Maurice, and Kenneth Rogoff. 2005. "The Unsustainable U.S. Current Account Revisited." *Proceedings of the Federal Reserve Bank of San Francisco*, February.

Prasad, Eswar. 2009. "Effects of the Financial Crisis on the U.S.-China Economic Relationship." *Cato Journal* 29, no. 2: 223–35.

Prasad, Eswar and Lei Ye. 2012. "Will the Renminbi Rule?" *Finance and Development*, March. http://www.brookings.edu/research/articles/2012/03/renminbi-rule-prasad.

Qiao, Hong. 2007. "Exchange Rate Changes and Trade Balances under the Dollar Standard." *Journal of Policy Modeling* 29:765–82.

Rajan, Raghuram G. 2010. *Fault Lines: How Hidden Fractures Still Threaten the World Economy*. Princeton, N.J.: Princeton University Press.

Roubini, Nouriel. 2005. "Global Imbalances: A Contemporary Rashomon Tale with Five Interpretations." Nouriel Roubini's Global Economics blog, http://roubiniglobal.com.

Schnabl, Gunther. 2010. "The Role of the Chinese Dollar Peg for Macroeconomic Stability in China and the World Economy." Working Papers on Global Financial Markets No. 13.

Schumpeter, Joseph. 1934. *The Theory of Economic Development: An Inquiry into Profits, Capital, Credit, Interest, and the Business Cycle*. Trans. Redvers Opie. Cambridge: Harvard University Press.

Subramanian, Arvind. 2011. *Eclipse: Living in the Shadow of China's Economic Dominance*. Washington, D.C.: Peterson Institute for International Economics.

Taylor, John B. 2009. *Getting Off Track*. Stanford, Calif.: Hoover Institution Press.

Triffin, Robert. 1960. *Gold and the Dollar Crisis: The Future of Convertibility*. New Haven: Yale University Press.

Wicksell, Knut. 1898. *Geldzins und Güterpreise: Eine Studie über die den Tauschwert des Geldes bestimmenden ursachen*. Jena: G. Fischer.

Zhou, Xiaochuan. 2009. "On Reforming the International Monetary System." People's Bank of China, March 23. News release.

INDEX